PURGED INTO HIS PURPOSE

By Pastor Timothy Moore

Be who God wants you
to be and nobody else

To Ella

Pastor Tim

Love ya!

Purged Into His Purpose

Editorial Services by:
The Scribes
649 Schaffer Road S. W.
Marietta, GA. 30060
E-mail:denisehj@msn.com

Acknowledgements

This Book is dedicated to my Invincible, Invisible, yet Visible Friend, The Bishop of faith and purging, CHRIST JESUS THE LORD. Also to my beautiful wife and praying partner, Lady Evelyn D. Moore, my wonderful children, and to the memory of two anointed parents, who are chillin-out in the presence of the Lord, Deacon Wallace and Martha J. Moore.

"**Purged Into His Purpose**" will cause you to examine the secret compartments of your life, stare destiny in the face and proceed with the plan of God. Too many of us are operating out of conjured up man-made plans that have been birthed out of frustration and our unwillingness to wait on God. This Book will unveil the secrets, encourage you to loose the chains of bondage, and strut into the promise. A very timely topic and a must-read for all who desire to awake from fantasy and live in truth.

-Bishop George G. Bloomer, Senior Pastor
Bethel Family Worship Center, Durham, NC

The Moment I saw Pastor Moore's book cover and title I knew this was a must book for the Body of Christ. When God showed up in our Church on January 19, 1997, His presence changed our lives forever. The process of purging that came prior to that moment was the cost that we as a Church and a people, had to pay.

But if purging brings us into His presence then, come Lord Jesus, and purge us again and again. Great book Pastor Moore!

-Bishop Bart Pierce, Senior Pastor
Rock City Church, Baltimore, MD

This book is composed of the dynamic, powerful, and anointed Word of God, which will equip you to expose the devil and the secret sins that plague your life. It will also give you insight on how to recognize, attack and conquer the enemy, as he tries to use everyday tactics to entrap us.

-Bishop Halton "Skip" Horton, Senior Pastor
Daystar Tabernacle, Douglasville, GA

Psalms 24:1-10

THE earth is the Lord's and all it contains,
The world, and those who dwell in it.

2   For He has founded it upon the seas,
and established it upon the rivers.

3   Who may ascend into the hill of the Lord?
And who may stand in His holy place?

4   He who has clean hands and a pure heart,
Who had not lifted up his soul to falsehood,
And has not sworn deceitfully.

5   He shall receive a blessing from the Lord
And righteousness from the God of his salvation.

6   This is the generation of those who seek Him,
Who seek thy face *–even* Jacob.   Selah.

7   Lift up your heads, O gates, And be lifted up, O ancient doors.
That the King of glory may come in.

8   Who is the King of glory?
The Lord strong and mighty,
The Lord mighty and battle.
9 Lift up your heads, O gates,
And lift *them* up, O ancient doors,
That the King of glory may come in!

10 Who is the King of glory?
The Lord of Hosts,He is the King of glory.   Selah.

Foreword

If I were asked to sum up the focus of my teachings or to identify the hallmark of my ministry in a single word or phrase, I would
have to say PURPOSE and DESTINY. For several decades, I have
preached sermons, written books and taught seminars that have
confronted, challenged and encouraged God's people to grasp the
absolute importance of being aligned with their divine purpose and
destiny. I have always stressed that only they as individuals can fulfill the specific calling God has placed on their life; That their indi-
vidual God-ordained destiny is the only thing that will truly satisfy
the deepest spiritual longings and desires of their heart and it is the
basis on which God will pass His eternal judgement. It is at this
point in my teaching that I will often refer to the passage of scripture in I Corinthians 3:10-15 that speaks about our works being
tested by God's fire – dead works are burned up; any good works
that survive the fire become the basis for eternal reward.

It gives me great pleasure to see my "son in the Lord" Pastor
Timothy Moore has received from the Lord a timely message and
has put it into a format that will reach and impact the Body of
Christ at this hour. PURGED INTO HIS PURPOSE is grounded
firmly in the Word of God and is filled with real life, up to the
minute examples that make it relevant and readable. Pastor Tim has
analyzed – in a most insightful fashion – the ways in which believers
are diverted from PURPOSE by intimacy with sin, secrecy and fantasy; by making covenants with darkness and dishonesty; by strongholds that grip the mind. But like any good author, he doesn't leave
the reader to wallow in guilt or self pity but shows – step by step,
scripture by scripture – how the DIVINE PURGING PROCESS
– God's fire – delivers the believer out of the deceptions of the
enemy and presses them as vessels of honor into the open arms of a
loving Heavenly Father. It is at this point that the sanctified
believer is free to PURSUE PURPOSE and enjoy a walk with the
Lord in DIVINE DESTINY.

– Bishop Don Meares

Introduction

Many people are experiencing spiritual pain, because the outer surroundings they live in do not match the inner image that was spoken by GOD into their spirits. So many in and out of the Church have become relational actors by keeping their composure in the midst of dissatisfaction. Understanding purpose is very important, but it is an essential requirement that we understand we must be Purged into the Purpose that GOD has designed for us. Having purpose without the knowledge of sanctification will deteriorate your spiritual DNA and you will become what people want you to be. We were not designed to have two identities, yet secret affairs with things done in the dark will cause you to have two personalities. There is a confidence that comes from purging that unlock treasures, which lead to purpose. The element that the Lord uses to purge with is fire. Fire separates that which is natural from that which is spiritual, wood, straw, and hay verses silver or gold which one are you? "Purged Into His Purpose" will unfold and help you to understand:

The Danger of a Life of Secrecy
The Power of Pain
The Power of Fire
The Beauty of Fire

And he shall sit as a refiner and purifier of silver: and he shall purify the sons of Levi, and purge them as gold and silver, that they may offer unto the Lord an offering in righteousness. Malachi 3:3

Table of Contents

A Secret Affair with Darkness

*"Therefore come out from them and be separate, says the Lord.
Touch no unclean thing, and I will receive you."*
(2 Corinthians 6:17 NIV)

Katherine and Jerry are both lead criminal defense lawyers in their firm. Katherine has worked there for 8 years, while Jerry just celebrated his 10th anniversary with the firm. They both worked their way up the ladder of success, struggling as they went from step to step. They walked over quite a few people as they climbed that ladder. Together, they successfully defended high profile cases and learned how to say the right things to please their executives while shifting the blame to others. They knew how to take the opportunity to make jokes at the expense of others, as well as laugh at their executives' jokes. They ate at the acceptable restaurants and socialized with the right people, while ostracizing others. The difference between Katherine and Jerry however, is that Katherine has a conscience. Jerry does not. When Katherine goes home at night she sometimes has a hard time sleeping because of some of the decisions she made at work that day. And when she visits her family for the holidays, even though her family dotes over her successful career, she often wonders if the price she's paying for it is too high.

You see, they knew that she had become a powerful attorney and was making a six-figure salary, but what they didn't know was that she traded in her morals to do so. The person they knew her to be was not the person who conferred with her clients, cut deals with the other attorneys, or entered the courtroom for every trial.

That was the side of her that they never saw. It was a side that she was not proud of either. She had gone farther than she ever anticipated when she took on a new personality to fit the job. Now she's finding that she can't live with the person she has become.

Since she began attending church again and reading the Word of God, it has become increasingly difficult for her to manipulate the jury when she gives her closing arguments. Sometimes she has haunting visions of the expressions on the victims' faces after a verdict is read that vindicates a client whom she knows is guilty. She even takes sleeping pills in an attempt to erase the images from her mind. She played all the games that people play when they try to succeed in the corporate world. Now she can't even look at herself in the mirror because every time she does she sees what she has become. You see, in the back of her mind she will always know who she is supposed to be-a mirror image of Jesus. Yet, when she looks in her mirror, what she sees doesn't even vaguely resemble Him.

Jerry on the other hand doesn't have a problem sleeping. His conscience was seared decades ago. The fact that he can defend people whom he knows are guilty of the crimes they are accused of doesn't bother him at all. He considers it a skill the way he twists the facts and distorts the truth to get his clients off. The way he sees it, he's just doing his job. After all, that's what he's getting paid for.

Katherine is like many Christians today. They go along just to get along and are uncomfortable during the entire ride. They become the people they think they have to be in order to succeed; yet they lose sight of who they really are. The truth is, they may not even know who they really are. They have an inside struggle. By day they are one person, but by night they are someone else. It's difficult to live that type of life because when you do you are living a lie, and sometimes you even confuse yourself. In the bible it tells us that we shall know the truth and the truth will make us free. (John 8:32)

If you find yourself in a similar situation to Katherine's, and you want to be free to be the person you were created to be, then this book is for you. You see, God has a purpose for every creature that exists on the face of this earth. Just take a look at the eco-system. There is an order to everything. When one element of nature gets out of balance it affects everything else. If the Creator of the universe pays that much attention to the mere physical elements that surround us, how much more attention do you think He is paying to his most precious creation, man? After all, He sent His only Son to die for us.

Yes He has a purpose for every human on the face of this earth. He has a purpose for Katherine and He has a purpose for you. The Bible says in Romans 8:28-29 that

"…We have been called according to his purpose. For those God foreknew, he also predestined to be conformed to the likeness of his Son, that he might be the first born among many brothers."

We were chosen, predestined before the foundation to this world to be conformed to His image. So how can we find our purpose and conform to the image of His Son? We must choose to do so.

We all have a will. God will not violate your will. God doesn't want puppets serving Him. God elected us, but we have the right to decline the position if we want to. If we refuse to be His, He will respect that choice. If we accept the call, He will give us the benefits that belong to every other member of His royal family, and He'll purge us so that we can fulfill our purpose.

In the next few chapters we will observe as Katherine sifts through the tangled web she's weaved to find her purpose. As she unravels the secrets of her world and allows the light of God's Word to shine on her identities, we will find out how she got into some of her situations and how you can get out of yours. Let's shatter the strongholds that have her bound to a life of misery and bring her to a place of peace. As we do, you will also find the keys that will unlock the doors to peace in your life. It's time for us to be set free from our secret identities so that we can enjoy life and be who God created us to be. God wants to purge us into His purpose.

Spiritual Schizophrenia

"To open their eyes and turn them from darkness to light, and from the power of Satan to God, so that they may receive forgiveness of sins and a place among those who are sanctified by faith in me."
(NIV Acts 26:18)

Jerry had just phoned Katherine's office and told her to prepare for a new client who would be meeting her within the next hour. There was an important manslaughter case that was coming to their firm. Katherine and Jerry were assigned to work on it as a team. As they met with their new client, they prepared their briefs, gathered the necessary information, and proceeded with the judicial process. The arraignment had already taken place and the trial date had been set.

Jerry handled the jury selection process. So you can imagine Katherine's surprise when she saw her pastor's wife in the jury stand on the first day of the trial. She froze and was almost unable to get out of her seat when it was time for her to give her opening statement. Her heart raced, her palms were sweaty. Could she display her usual courtroom personality in front of the Pastors' wife?

Sis. Grace was stunned to see Katherine as one of the attorneys on the case. She recalled how repentant Katherine was as she prayed with her at the altar. She had rededicated her life to the Lord about two years earlier. On that day, Katherine bared her soul before the Lord. Sis. Grace had only known her on a casual basis. She had noticed how faithfully Katherine gave to the financial needs of the ministry, such as the congregation's Battered Women's

Shelter. She also recalled how supportive Katherine was with her "Amen's," while the pastor preached his Sunday sermons.

Meanwhile, Katherine's mind drifted back to the first time she met Sis. Grace and Pastor Mark. She had held them in such high esteem that she didn't want to do anything that would cause them to be disappointed with her. She had admired their commitment to God and how consistent they were no matter what the situation was. Deep down in her heart she wondered if she would ever be like that. Whenever she was in church she made sure she said the right things and acted the right way. She even made sure she said, "Amen" at the right times and shouted when the Spirit moved her. This situation was different though. She was no longer in church-on Sis. Grace's playing field. She was in a different arena. This was her turf and the rules of the game were different. Or were they?

While sitting there an uneasy feeling came over her. All of a sudden she became confused. How would Sis. Grace view Katherine's defense in this trial? Yes this was her job, and she did it well. That's how she made it to the top. But would Sis. Grace find her tactics a little unethical, or un-Christ-like? "Katherine, Katherine," Jerry called as the judge motioned for the defense to proceed with their opening statement. "You're up." After that session ended Jerry pulled Katherine aside and asked her what was wrong. He told her that she wasn't as forceful and dynamic as she usually is. She apologized and assured him that she would be back to her normal self for the next court session.

For the first time in Katherine's career, she admitted to herself that she was having a secret affair with darkness. Somehow she had weaved a web of deceit and she didn't know what to do. She was living one life in front of the members of her church, and another one on the job. She never considered the possibility that those two lifestyles would one day collide. Could she keep up the charade?

Conviction overwhelmed her when she saw Sis. Grace sitting in front of her. The light of Jesus in Sis. Grace shined on

Katherine's secret life of darkness. For that minute space in time she saw herself the way she really was, entangled in a web of deceit. What was she going to do? How was she going to handle it? Would she be able to keep up her church image while Sis. Grace was in this courtroom and still win her case? How did she ever get caught in such a secret affair with darkness in the first place?

Secret Fantasies

*"If we say we have no sin, we deceive ourselves,
and the truth is not in us."*
1 John 1:8

Secrets can be quite alluring. In Katherine's case, the devil lured her into a life of secrecy by presenting her with a false image and making it look appealing. She knew that some of the decisions she was making concerning her career were wrong. But the enemy told her that no one had to know about them. No one would ever find out as long as she kept them secret. Katherine fell prey to the enemy's trap and began a secret affair with darkness.

Unfortunately, secret affairs are nothing new to us. They are all too common. We see stories on television and in the movies about people who have secret affairs and live two separate lives all the time. We've even heard news reports of individuals who to some degree, have gotten away with living double lives. They hid their lifestyles from their families and friends for years.

Secrets have the power to entice unsuspecting people like Katherine into their world because they possess an important element-a fantasy. A fantasy is an unreal expectation about a thing or person. Fantasy, fan, fantasize, they all contain the same root word. Fantasies make secrets exciting and give them power. That's the devil's trick. A person who fantasizes is one who daydreams about something that isn't real. The key word here is unreal. Seldom do people who fantasize understand that their dreams are just that, dreams. They have a hard time distinguishing the dream from reality. Fans have difficulty coming to grips with reality too.

So if you are a fan of a person, you have an unreal expectation of that person-a fantasy. On the other hand, if a person is a fan of yours, their expectation of you is unreal too.

One thing about fantasies is that they only happen in the secrecy of your mind. No one will ever know you have fantasies unless you tell someone about them. A fantasy cannot be seen with the eye. It only occurs in the imagination. So you can't see the evidence of one's fantasies unless you observe a person's actions.

Katherine was enticed to make it to the top of her law firm by one of fantasy's temptations. A fantasy has three temptations-prosperity, prestige, or pleasure. These are the elements of fantasy that entrap us. Katherine had formed certain pictures in her mind about how things would be if she were one of the leading lawyers in the firm. She imagined the glamour, glitter and glory that she would have. Had she stopped and compared those images with the Word of God, she would have been able to count the costs and see that they were just a part of a fantasy. That's not to say that God didn't want her to be promoted in her career, He did. She just didn't do it His way.

You see, the world tells you that if you want to be promoted to the top you have to kiss up, sleep around, and be dishonest. God's Word doesn't agree with those methods. Those were the images that were presented to Katherine and she bought the package. She accepted them and made them a part of her fantasy.

Consider what might have happened had Katherine chosen to succeed God's way. The Bible tells us that

"For the eyes of the Lord range throughout the earth to strengthen those whose hearts are fully committed to him." (2 Chronicles 16:9 NIV)

Katherine could have had it all from God, but she settled for a whole lot less.

She focused on the images that the world presented to her. Yet God tells us what to do with the images in our minds in 2

Corinthians 10:4-5.

"The weapons we fight with are not the weapons of the world. On the contrary, they have divine power to demolish strongholds. We demolish arguments and every pretension that sets itself up against the knowledge of God, and we take captive every thought to make it obedient to Christ." (NIV)

We are to destroy every image that enters our minds and doesn't agree with God's Word. We can't let fantasies control us. If they do, we can't live according to our purposes.

Unfortunately, we live in a world where fantasies run rampant. People fantasize about the images of popular stars, athletes, and musical artists or just about anybody you could name. But those images aren't real. Those images don't reflect the real character of those persons. They are the images that the media wants you to see and they are pumped up-exaggerated.

When God's people begin to focus on images other than the ones God has given us in His Word we get into trouble. Yet the Word clearly tells us what to focus our minds on.

"Finally, brothers, whatever is true, whatever is noble, whatever is right, whatever is pure, whatever is lovely, whatever is admirable- if anything is excellent or praiseworthy think about such things." (Philippians 3:8 NIV)

Apparently, Katherine wasn't keeping her mind on the Word of God, or she wouldn't have been able to continue to be deceived by that life of secrecy. She became trapped by one of the elements of fantasy and was led into an affair with darkness. You see, the only way to maintain an affair with darkness is to consistently shut out the light of God's Word. That means that she had to focus her attention on the affairs of this world's system and the lies that the enemy presented to her instead of God's Word. However, Katherine isn't the only person who has fallen into that trap. Let's look at some people in the Bible who fell for it too.

Fantasy's Deceit

Take Eve, for instance. In Genesis 3: 1 it says,
*"Now the serpent was more crafty than any of the wild animals the
Lord God had made. He said to the woman, "Did God really say,
'You must not eat from any tree in the garden'?" (NIV)"*

The devil got Eve to focus on something she shouldn't have focused on. God told them not to eat of the fruit. Yet, when Eve continued to allow her attention to be drawn to it she began to desire it. When you focus on something too long, you begin to fantasize about it. You imagine things about it that are not real. If you continue to focus on it you will eventually act on it. The more you continue to act on it the better you become with it and the more you desire it. It is this process that causes some people to become addicts and fanatics.

Once Eve began focusing on the fruit, she started to wonder what it would taste like and what would happen if she did eat it-pleasure. Pleasure is one of fantasy's temptations. As she fantasized about the pleasure she would have if she ate the fruit she began to covet it. Exodus 20:17 tells us, *"You shall not covet..."* The word covet used here is *epithumeo* and it means "to set the heart upon; long for; lust after; to long for, passionately, to breath hard." When your mind is fixed on a particular thing. It causes you to long for it and breath harder. The more Eve looked, the more she longed after it, and it got her into trouble.

Do you see Katherine's situation in this picture? She became entangled in that web of deceit when she began to fantasize about the pleasure she would enjoy if she bent the rules a little as she pursued her career. She coveted some things that were not good for her. So, if you want to avoid a situation like Eve and Katherine's set your mind on things that are above, not those things that will decay on this earth.

If you're going to fantasize then you must make sure that you fantasize about the right thing, the right way. Don't allow your heart to fantasize and entertain conduct that violates the characteristics of the anointing. Do like David did. In Psalm 42:1 it says, *"As the deer pants for streams of water, so my soul pants for you, O God." (NIV)* He coveted the anointing. His heart panted after a relationship with God. If you want to fantasize, do it this way. *Pant* means "to covet, to desire God."

When was the last time that Jesus made your heart beat real fast? When was the last time that your heart ran away and you had to catch it because it was chasing God? See, we fantasize about all these different guys and girls who take our minds places we shouldn't go. We imagine ourselves doing things we shouldn't-with people we shouldn't-without considering the consequences. I'd rather fantasize about something that's real, not something foolish.

God's love for me is real. I can't wait to get to God. I can't wait till I get to my private closet and put my arms around the Lord. If your heart beats for God you can't wait. You want to read the Word and get down on your knees. Let God turn you on. You're looking for the right person, that special one. God will let you know that there's something about Him that you haven't met in anyone else in your life. God's got my nose wide open; I'm in love. You can fall in love with God too. Desire to fellowship with Him.

Eve fell prey to another temptation of fantasy in the Garden of Eden. The devil offered Eve no limitations on what she could have in the garden. That meant that she would be in the position to be equal with God-prestige. What Eve didn't realize was that she was already just like God. God made men a little lower than Himself. Hebrews 2:6-7 says,

"What is man that you are mindful of him, the son of man that you care for him? You made him a little lower than the angels; you crowned him with glory and honor and put everything under his feet." (NIV)

He had given Adam and Eve dominion, power, and authority over every creature on the face of the earth. Inside of themselves they had the same abilities that were in their Father. He gave them the power to speak His Word just like He does, and see what they say come to pass in their lives. They were His son and daughter. No other creature on the face of the earth had those abilities. How much more prestigious can a person get?

And if you want to consider their prosperity, all of their needs were meet. They didn't want for anything. They were surrounded by gold, precious gems, and all the food they needed. They lived in paradise.

Neither Eve nor Katherine knew what was theirs in God. They both became victims of fantasy. They were lured away from the truth of God's Word. However, once they began to live out their fantasies, they had to do so under the cover of darkness. Eve had to hide from God, and Katherine was trying to keep her other personality a secret.

When they allowed something secret to go on in their minds it provided a warm dark place for the seeds of that thought to germinate. And once those seeds germinate they take on a life of their own and they choke the real you out. They also choke out the word (Mk. 4:19).

When you open your mind to the darkness of secrecy there are consequences. Notice, After Adam and Eve sinned they hid from themselves one another. They covered their nakedness. Then they hid themselves from God. When you hid like that something has happened. Secrecy causes you to focus on the nakedness and make you isolate yourself from others and God. You lose freedom and the ability to know yourself intimately. Then when the light comes you can't even face yourself. If you hide from yourself too long then after a while you don't even know yourself. Now without even realizing it, Katherine had fostered two personalities.

"This is the verdict: Light has come into the world, but men loved darkness instead of light because their deeds were evil.

Everyone who does evil hates the light, and will not come into the light for fear that his deeds will be exposed.

But whoever lives by the truth comes into the light, so that it may be seen plainly that what he has done had been done through God."

John 3:18-21

Dr. Jekyll and Ms. Hyde
No one who wants to become a public figure acts in secret.
Since you are doing these things, show yourself to the world.
(John 7:4 NIV)

Katherine chose to live a secret life. The word secret used in the Old Testament is cether. It means, "to hide by covering." The New Testament word for secret is kruptos, and it means, "to conceal or inwardly hide information." Katherine did both. She hid the person she really was and took on a character that was not hers. It was a gradual process, situation by situation, a little at a time. She let her guard down as she was enticed by the world. The world tries to pull you into its methods. It's part of the world's way of doing things to live in secrecy.

She had two identities-Dr. Jekyll and Ms. Hyde. By day she was Dr. Jekyll, and by night she was Ms. Hide. On Sundays she was the devout Christian who eagerly participated in the church's activities. But from Mondays to Saturdays she was the ruthless lawyer who broke every moral standard she could in order to stay at the top of her firm and win.

Does it sound familiar? We've got people who can stand in the pulpit and preach by day, but at night they have an affair with Sister "So-n-so" in the choir. God help us! They are Clark Kent by day, but as soon as the lights go down they go into the phone booth and change into Superman. But you know what, that's a lot of work-trying to be something by night and then remembering who you are by day. For a minute in that courtroom Katherine forgot who she was.

In order to live a life of secrecy you must bury the truth. Katherine had done it subconsciously for so long that she didn't notice it until the light of God's Word shined on her secret. In order to get that job she felt she had to maintain a certain image. Then a little later on she felt she needed to do something else to keep or advance in that position. Even though she may have questioned the suggested image, she conformed to it and said to herself, "I can do that too." Before she realized it she had taken on another personality.

To accept the hidden things of dishonesty is normal to the world. To be secret is normal. Not to have a secret life is abnormal. Look at the soap operas. They are full of lies and secrets. That's the lifestyle that the enemy is trying to put on the people of God. And Katherine accepted that lifestyle and played the game by their rules. So she said, "I can do that." Yet that personality wasn't representative of the Katherine God created and chose. When she saw Sis. Grace in that courtroom, it was as though she was looking into the mirror of God's Word. And she didn't see a reflection of Jesus at all. She saw a Katherine she could no longer live with.

You see, Katherine tried to block out the light of the Son as long as she could. The problem with secrets is that secrecy eclipses-blocks-the light of the Son that shines on the shameful things of our lives. Shame will say, "Eclipse that light. Block it." And you will do whatever you need to do to block that light, and keep that thing hidden. But when you conceal your issues from that light something else is happening. Decay is living off of the darkness that secrecy provides. There is decay that is going on in your life. Slowly, but surely that secret is eating away at you. Whether it is physically, mentally, spiritually, emotionally, or financially your secret is taking its toll. Secrecy can only feed off of darkness; it can't feed off of light. Anything going on in your life that is secret has got to feed off of darkness, not light. The word of God tells us that men love darkness rather than light because their deeds are evil. You keep that thing hidden because you know it isn't what it should be.

A part of you wants to expose the secret, but evil will tell you not to go to God with your secrets. Instead, secrecy encourages you to conceal them from Him. Perhaps you are afraid that if you go to God and be honest about this thing somebody is going to make you feel bad; you're going to be ashamed. So you accept that lie and the secret continues to eat away at you.

This leads to the disintegration of character and personality. You begin to ignore your morals-your conscience-when it warns you about right and wrong. It affects every part of your life. Sometimes when you come to church you can't get loose and feel the Holy Ghost. That's because you're taking too much work to try to hide the other person that you have created. Sin offends the light that is in you. And the Spirit of God convicts you of your sin so it's hard to worship unless you are ready to repent. The only way you can hide that other person is to lie.

You may even see somebody at church who says, "You know, I thought I saw you somewhere." And you might say, "No that was-n't me." Once you tell one lie you have to tell another one to cover up the first lie that you told. It is a continuous process that weaves an entangling web. Before you realize it, you are the other person. The real you only comes out when it is safe. Your personality has made the adjustment so that you can continue to hide your secret. But a secret can only be kept for so long. It's coming out whether you like it or not. The light was shining on Katherine's secret in the courtroom that day. God was waiting to free her from the grip of darkness and purge her to His purpose.

The truth is that if Katherine ever let the truth be resurrected it will free her from the bondage of a secret life. John. 8:32 tells us, *"Then you will know the truth, and the truth will make you free."* The anointing is truth and it will make you free. It was the lie that got her into bondage in the first place just like it was a lie that got Eve into trouble in Eden.

I'm sure you can recall situations in your life when you became a servant to secrecy. It was the lie that told you that you could feel good in the morning. It was the lie that told you all you had to do was take a little sniff right now; you could get high and everything would be all right. It was a lie that told you to do whatever you had to do to get that job. It was the lie that said you could be in one type of conversation outside of the presence of your husband or wife and then in their presence you had to do it another way. It was a lie, and you can't even blame that on the devil. You listened to it and got involved in something that God told you not to be involved in, in the first place. It is the lie that makes you have more respect for persons than you do for God and His house. The devil presents the temptation to us and then lies to us. He tries to get us to succumb to it. God always makes a way out, but the choice is ours.

There's another character in the Bible who fell prey to the temptations of fantasy and became entangled in a secret world of darkness just as Katherine did. David also had a fantasy and was captivated by the imaginations of his heart. (2 Samuel 11th and 12th chapters) He saw Bathsheba bathing on her roof and coveted her. So he sent for her and slept with her. Bathsheba became pregnant. Then to hide his sin he tried to get her husband Uriah-who was away at war-to sleep with her. So he called him in from the battle. When Uriah wouldn't sleep with his wife while his comrades were fighting, David sent him back to the battle along with a message to his commander. The message said that Uriah should be put on the front lines of the battle. Uriah died there. He was killed in order to cover up David's sin.

David's first sin was to covet another man's wife. His second was to sleep with her. His third was to kill her husband. Each time he committed one sin he had to commit another just to cover up the last one. We see how David became proud because he figured out how to hide his sins.

David committed those sins for the feeling. Everybody likes to feel good. But he had wives all over the place and he didn't need another one. David wasn't supposed to go somewhere else to get what he was supposed to be getting at home. See the devil can set up an artificial assembly. He has one for every need you have. When people get hooked on drugs they are trying to feel spiritual. That's the devil's counterfeit. But that wasn't David's only problem. God was trying to get through to David, but he had become so good at hiding his secrets, that he couldn't even see his sin himself.

A Web of Deceit

"You did it in secret, but I will do this thing in broad daylight before all Israel."
(2 Samuel 12:12- NIV)

There's always the temptation to take that road and resist what God is saying to you. Let me show you how your character changes. David was so involved in another man's character that he was keeping that man separate from the man he really was. He was into that secrecy so deep that he didn't even know he had another character. Second Samuel 12:5 says that the prophet Nathan had to deliver a message to David. While delivering this message Nathan told David a story about a rich man who had several sheep of his own, but one night a guest came to visit him. Instead of killing one of his flock, he took the sheep that belonged to his neighbor. It was the only one his neighbor had. David became angry and said that the guilty man should be punished. Nathan pointed out to him that he was that man. He had taken the only wife Uriah had.

It was then that David realized that he was in trouble. Until this point David had gone on and lived his life unaware of how much his life had eroded. Until that moment he wasn't aware of the decay. He was almost schizophrenic. This wasn't a sin that David did one time and refused to repent for. It was something that he hidden over a process of time. He hid this sin for months. By the time God sent Nathan to confront him, the baby was about to be born. That's what happened to Katherine too. She had played the role for years. As a matter of fact, her courtroom personality was so established that she wasn't even aware who she was anymore. It wasn't until she saw Sis. Grace sitting in the courtroom that she had a reality check.

Nathan's message was David's reality check. When he had his affair with Bathsheba, no one else knew about it. David was hiding his secret under the cover of darkness. The Word of God says that men love darkness rather than light because they are hiding evil deeds. Secrets can only be kept under the cover of darkness. When the light hits them they are revealed. That's why God sent the prophet Nathan to him. God said you did it in secret, I'll proclaim it in the open.

Psalm 51:1-13
Have mercy on me, O God, according to your unfailing love; according to your great compassion blot out my transgressions.
Wash away all my iniquity and cleanse me from my sin.
For I know my transgressions, and my sin is always before me.
Against you, you only, have I sinned and done what is evil in your sight, so that you are proved right when you speak and justified when you judge.
Surely I have been a sinner from birth, sinful from the time my mother conceived me.
Surely you desire truth in the inner parts; you teach me wisdom in the inmost place.
Cleanse me with hyssop, and I will be clean; wash me, and I will be whiter than snow.
Let me hear joy and gladness; let the bones you have crushed rejoice.
Hide your face from my sins and blot out all my iniquity.
Create in me a pure heart, O God, and renew a steadfast spirit within me.
Do not cast me from your presence or take your Holy Spirit from me. Restore to me the joy of your salvation and grant me a willing spirit, to sustain me.

Then I will teach transgressor you ways, and sinners will turn back to you.

Saving Grace

Make no mistake about it; God is not out to get us. It is His mercy and grace-His love for us that causes Him to shine the light on our secret affairs with darkness. If we submit our affairs of darkness to His light He will deal with them and give us grace. When we deal with those issues God will take that truth and make people see our faults in another way. Nobody can do that but God. It's time to come out of our secret lives of darkness and walk in the light of God's Word. It's time for us to be real and tell the truth. However, if we don't and He has to handle them, we'll be in trouble because He will expose us. See, whatever is done in the dark will be put out in the light. Romans 2:16 says that God shall judge the secrets of men by Jesus Christ-the anointing in you. God was trying to take David and Katherine somewhere. He had something special for them, but they could not receive it until they had been purged from the secrets they kept in darkness.

While David lived this life of secrecy, his bones waxed old all day long. He had gotten sick from holding the secret on the inside so long. The moisture, the vitality, and fire had gone out of his life. The lifestyle of sin that he lived while hiding that secret passed on to his family. It brought destruction and heartache. However, when he acknowledged his sin God immediately forgave him. Bring that secret to God and He'll forgive you and put the life back into your ministry, marriage, and finances as soon as you do.

Jesus is coming to light up everything that you have that isn't right. If you are having a secret affair, or you're enslaved by pornography give it to Jesus. If you listen for that beep on your beeper from your special girlfriend-that special signal, and you know how to get to the phone at the right time give it to God. I'm sure you've never thought about it, but guess who is at the phone with you? As you get to the phone at the right time, let me tell you who is standing right there with you. His name is Jesus! He knows what is going on in the darkness. Don't let your life and your family be destroyed because of some secret.

Throw the light on that thing. Blind the devil because he doesn't like light. Be what God called you to be. Be honest with yourself. You can hold something secret in the dark, but while you do your bones are getting rotten; your lifestyle is being sucked up alive. No one else may know what's going on, but the Word of God does.

"The word of God is living and active. Sharper than any double-edged sword, it penetrates even to dividing soul and spirit, joints and marrow; it judges the thoughts and attitudes of the heart." (Hebrews 4:12 NIV)–Amplified instead.

The word of God knows. All things are naked and open to Him. It's time for us to see where the real life is. If we call ourselves Christians we need to live like Jesus Christ.

You see, what Katherine and David didn't realize is that a life of secrecy and living in darkness diminishes your power. One of the most powerful men in the Bible found that out the hard way. Take a look a Samson. He was a Nazarite and was supposed to abstain from certain things according to his vow. He was to keep himself clean and not cut his hair. He had the same vow that Jesus had. Yet Samson gave himself away to the devil. He was supposed to overthrow the Philistines. But as soon as he tried to enjoy what everybody else enjoyed, as soon as he started compromising his position and ignoring what God told him to do, he lost his ministry. So many Christians today find themselves in the similar situations, but it's time for the body of Christ to come out from those who are encouraging us to enjoy darkness. We should not be people who are ducking and dodging the light. There are consequences to dodging the light.

When you live in darkness the devil is setting you up and you don't even know it. Look at Samson. You'd think he would have awaken and seen it coming. (Judges chapter 16) He should have caught on to what Delilah was trying to do. Three times she played this game with him and he never figured it out. The first time Delilah asked about his strength's source she woke him up and said, "Samson, the Philistines are upon you!" And he broke loose. This happened again and again. But this was just God's grace, giving him time to get it right. God was making a way out for him and he wouldn't take it. God was saying, "Get it right before I have to deal with you."

Meanwhile, Delilah was saying, "Three strikes and you're out." She asked him, "How are you going to say you love me when your heart isn't with me?" She pressed him daily with her words so that his soul was vexed. This was the devil getting to him. She was working on him with her words. You can be in a situation that you know you shouldn't be in, and it will vex you so, that you feel like you are going to die. That's what happened to Samson. So he finally shared all his heart with her.

All of us have secrets so you'd better wake up. Don't tell the devil what your weak point is. The only way he'll know is you've got to tell him. He's not omniscient like God. The only way the devil will know your secret is if you say it to somebody.

"There are three things that are too amazing for me, four that I do not understand:

The way of an eagle in the sky, the way of a snake on a rock, the way of a ship on the high seas, and the way of a man with a maiden.

This is the way of an adulteress: She eats and wipes her mouth and says, "I've done nothing wrong." (Proverbs 30:18-20-NIV)

The Dangers of Secrecy
*"This will take place on the day when God will judge men's
secrets through Jesus Christ, as my gospel declares."*
(Romans 2:16-NIV)

After he told her all his heart the Philistines came up to her and
put the money in her hand. It was a set up. Somebody may be setting you up. When you are dealing with darkness they really don't
care anything about you. After she finished her job and his strength
left him, she was gone too. But he lost something much more valuable than Delilah. He didn't even realize it, but God's grace was
gone too. Some people don't even know when God's grace is gone.
Samson had just reaped the consequences of sin.

Samson said, "I will get up as at other times and shake myself."
When he tried this time, he realized that he only had the strength
of an ordinary man. God didn't leave him, but the anointing was
gone. That's how the devil traps God's children when they continue to practice sin. Then when the anointing leaves the devil comes
in and says, "I finally got you where I wanted you." And then-Pow!
A note comes in the mail that says the AIDS test was positive.
AIDS eats people up alive. Die? Your mind is messed up. Then
when the note comes you remember the times when you had the
chance to get away from it. We can't play around with sin. We can't
play with it. These people don't care anything about your life. The
devil puts some people in place to try and take you out. This is seri-
ous business. It's time to put your life under control and submit it
to Jesus.

God said, "I'm giving you another chance to get it right. I've

26

got time. My mercy is from everlasting to everlasting." Yet what we can't see is that we have become intoxicated off of the juice that comes from the grapes of secrecy. Studies show that 80% of the affairs happen on jobs, and the other 20% comes from churches. Now what's wrong with that picture? The deception of pleasure makes a life of secrecy attractive. Samson was deceived by it too. He let Delilah console him. Yet how can the devil console you? It should have been obvious to him that Delilah wasn't on his team. She persuaded him to overcome his conscience and join her in an affair with darkness. By participating in this he risked the wrath of his conscience and sold his convictions for free. When we purposely disobey God's Word, we do the same thing. Yielding to the temptation may be sweet at first, but at the end it will be bitter. God said don't you know that the demons are haunting the scene waiting for the anointing to leave you when you step out there and do what I told you not to do? Then they accuse you before God, and they wait for the opportunity to take you down. We go ahead and take whatever miseries sin offers instead of God's best when we disobey God. This includes both here on earth in after death. Sin will bring you misery every time. You might get by for a little while, but you won't get away with it.

Don't let anybody fool you. A lot of people fall by the wayside because they took their eyes off of God. When the light comes you must accept the truth of His Word. "For you a holy people to the Lord your God; the Lord your God has chosen you to be a people for His own possession out of all the peoples who are on the face of the earth. Deut. 7:6. You need to put your hands up and give Him praise for giving you another chance.

The devil's purpose is to keep you from receiving what God has for you. Harboring sin only prevents you from receiving God's best-His purpose for your life. But openness before God, living good, gives you confidence in Jesus, you feel you can run through troops. David realized this though. He remembered what his life was once like when his heart was pure before God. He recalled the times when the power of God was with him and the anointing was on his life. He remembered the victories he enjoyed-the lion, the bear, Goliath, his many battles, God delivering him from Saul.

All this changed when he stopped going out to battle. When he stayed at home he had an idol mind. That's when the enemy got in. He didn't monitor his thought life. He succumbed to vain imaginations and thoughts that did not agree with the Word of God. This caused his downfall.

Romans 8:5-9 Those who live according to the sinful nature have their minds set on what that nature desires; but those who live in accordance with the Spirit have their minds set on what the Spirit desires.

The mind of sinful man is death, but the mind controlled by the Spirit is life and peace,

Because the sinful mind is hostile to God. It does not submit to God's law, nor can it do so

Those controlled by the sinful nature cannot please God.

You, however are controlled not by the sinful nature but by the Spirit, if the Spirit of God lives in you.

Imaginations of the Heart

*So I say, live by the Spirit, and you will not gratify the
desires of the sinful nature.*
(Galatians 5:16-NIV)

An imagination is the act of forming a mental image of something never experienced in reality. The images you form in your
imagination can be of things that may be real or unreal. The difference between an imagination and a fantasy is that a fantasy is
extravagant, fictitious, whimsical, inconsistent, and unstable. God
gave us our imaginations so that we would have a tool we can use
to envision the things He has for us. In order to have faith you
must have an imagination. After all, Jesus said

"...Whatever you ask for in prayer, believe that you have
received it, and it will be yours." (Mark 11:24 NIV) It takes an
imagination to believe you have something that you can't confirm
with your physical senses. You can't see, taste, touch, hear, or smell
it. Without an imagination, you wouldn't be able to exercise your
faith.

However, the enemy can molest our imaginations just like someone molests a kid. He can put people in your life who see your vul-
nerabilities and can tell that you are open to them. They violate
your imagination by trying to make you accept theirs and make it
your own. They do this by distorting the image of the truth and
creating a false sense of reality in your mind. And you accept yourself the way they see you, not the way God made you.

Have you ever seen yourself in a false way? Perhaps you imagined that you were the queen of America, or the King of England.

If so, you just limited yourself. God said, "I was going to make you the king of the world." Katherine opened up herself to Jerry's image of her. She saw herself as weak, unable to win a case without manipulating the system and using unethical methods. What she didn't see was a person who had God in her corner. She couldn't see the favor of God on her life. Nor was she aware that if she lived in the light of His Word she would be the head, not the tail in her business. God would put her above, never beneath if she obeyed His commandments. Blessings would run her down and overtake her if she saw herself the way God created her to be. He would position her to have all of the prestige, prosperity, and power that belong to His children. But she didn't understand that. Instead, she traded in her faith for the devil's imagination.

The devil tries to fool you and give you his imagination so that you will not trust your faith. And you fall for it when you don't have a secure foundation on the Word of God. Then you start believing his imagination-the picture that's in the devil's mind. That's the form that you begin to take on instead of what God said you were. So the image that you take on is an imagination of the enemy instead of the faith of God that's supposed to be released in your life. Now your conscience has got to be purged because your imagination really isn't yours; you're captive at the devil's will. God can't take you into the life He has for you because there are too many impurities there. There's too much junk inside the minds of God's children for him to move the way He wants to move. That's why the body of Christ doesn't have the Power of Jesus. We don't have the faith to be who He called us to be. That's because faith can't come except you hear by the Word of God. Rom. 10:17

There's a lesson to be learned from this. God will talk to you about your situation. God didn't send Jesus to condemn the world, but if you as a member of the body of Christ are going to fulfill your purpose, you must allow the light to shine on your secret affairs of darkness. You are individually responsible to get to your purpose. You should want the skeletons out of your closet so that you can be all that God created you to be. God chose you and put His special word on you. The devil doesn't want you to reach it. If you are about to get to your purpose in life the devil is upset. He's unleashed a brand new warfare in the spirit now. We have to be ready to fight in the spirit realm and win this battle. This is a new day. Christ wants to return for His body. Yet the body of Christ isn't ready for Christ to return. We're not pure enough.

Look at David, Eve, Katherine and Samson. The images of the enemy split their minds. James talks about a double minded man. He says that they are unstable in all their ways. They were unstable. Shall I go to the left or the right? Shall I be phony today or be real? Am I Dr. Jekyll or Mr. Hyde? But God wants you to walk straight, not to the left or the right. If you do, then you'll be prosperous and content. When you live holy, the way God wants you to live; He will not withhold any good thing from you. His Word tells us that. If you've got a limp in your walk it will hold up your blessings. But I dare you to walk straight up. God said, "I won't hold back your blessing, your healing, power, peace, might, strength, or finances." I've got my walk now. Do you have yours? I'm walking upright now. It's time for us to pull ourselves back together and face the music. Become one person. (Proverbs. 6:23)

To do so, you'll have to break lose from the grip that the secrets of darkness are holding you in. Can you earnestly say, "Lord, I want you to uncover my secret affair with darkness and teach me who I really am?" If you can then you are ready for the next step in finding and living out your purpose-the purging process.

Psalm 32:1-8

Blessed is he whose transgressions are for given, whose sins are covered.
Blessed is the man whose sin the Lord does not count against him and in whose spirit is no deceit.

When I kept silent, my bones wasted away through my groaning all day long.
For day and night your hand was heavy upon me; my strength was sapped as in the heat of summer. Selah
Then I acknowledged my sin to you and did not cover up my iniquity. I said, "I will confess my transgressions to the Lord"- and you forgave the guilt of my sin.
Therefore let everyone who is godly pray to you while you may be found; surely when the mighty waters rise, they will not reach him.
You are my hiding place; you will protect me from trouble and surround me with songs of deliverance Selah
I will instruct you and teach you in the way you should go;' I will counsel you and watch over you.

The Cleansing Light

Purge isn't a word you hear used too often. Most of the time you only hear older adults use it when they talk about constipation. A laxative helps you to purge, clean out any blockages in your system. Well as Christians, sometimes we have spiritual blockages in our systems that need to be cleaned out too. See, God has all these wonderful things in store for you, but you can't receive them because there is something in the way. God wants to move every hindrance out of the way so that you can receive His best. In order to do that He must purge your conscience from everything that is not like Him and give you a revelation of His purpose for your life.

The word purge is *zaqaq* and it means "to remove opponents that cause guilt, by conflict of devotion; to systematically have the spiritual bowels deleted of unwanted and unneeded impurities, which are in opposition to God." Being purged indicates a state of heart where there is complete devotion to God. As unadulterated water is pure, and gold without alloy is pure gold, so is the heart that is undivided. It has no conflict of loyalties, no cleavage of interests, no mixture of motives, no hypocrisy and no insecurity.

You must release everything in your spirit that has nothing to do with Him.

So how can you have your conscience purged? Hebrews 9:14 says,

"How much more, then, will the blood of Christ, who through the eternal Spirit offered himself unblemished to God, cleanse our consciences from acts that lead to death, so that we may serve the living God!"

Let the blood of Jesus wash your conscience unto good works.

As you may recall, earlier we discussed how the light of the Word shined on the secrets of darkness and exposed them. It is that same light that washes them and gives you new, clear direction for your life. This light of the Word will reveal things to you about yourself that you weren't even aware of. By now I'm sure you know that you are a king or a queen in God's kingdom. The question is why didn't you know it before?

There are several reasons for this. One is that when your heart has not been purged, and the enemy can stop the revelation in your life about yourself. The revelation gives you light. The enemy doesn't want you to have the light. He wants you walking in darkness. He likes it when you accept the hidden things of dishonesty. That's why when God starts working on your life the way He desires, the devil will send people as sources of persecution to you. Somebody is going to call you crazy. He doesn't want you to handle the things that are hidden. He wants you to try and keep them concealed. He knows that you can't commend yourself to every man's conscience when yours isn't right. Yet God has called us to renounce "...secret and shameful ways..." You must understand that

"...We do not use deception, nor do we distort the word of God; On the contrary, by setting forth the truth plainly we commend ourselves to every man's conscience in the sight of God." (2 Corinthians 4:2 NIV)

The devil wants you to go for what everyone else goes for. He wants you to accept the hidden things of dishonesty and be normal. When you walk in the light you are abnormal. To walk in the light is also to go from the flesh realm into the spirit. As you do this you begin to reflect the image of your brother Jesus. Remember, they called Him crazy too. Don't let that bother you though. When people call you unbalanced you've just begun to live. Don't go the same way everybody else is going. Go in the opposite direction.

We've been making covenants with darkness too long. This is the season to renounce the hidden things of dishonesty. We've been living in the flesh. It is time to get rid of the toys that the enemy has used to set us up with. If we get where we're supposed to be then we'll understand things about ourselves that will make us run to God.

Another reason may be that you are not careful what you expose yourself to. We're living inside of a spiritual world and you've got to guard your heart. You've got to watch what you do. You can't do what everybody else does. You have to avoid evil-"poneros," foulness, flaws. That's where we get the word pornography-"evil writing." The only thing that can cure the disease of pornerous is light. Avoid the evil and live in the light.

God anointed our ears and said, you'd better watch what goes in your ears, and he anointed our mouths and said you'd better watch what comes out of your mouth. You'd better quit hanging around those who are talking about things that don't have anything to do with God. When you hang with them what's happening is you aren't being separate. You're being just like them. As Christians we aren't even supposed to have certain things mentioned among us. God commanded us to

"...Come out from them and be separate... Touch no unclean thing, and I will receive you. I will be a Father to you, and you will be my sons and daughters, says the Lord Almighty." (2 Corinthians 6:17-18)

Yet sometimes there is no distinction between the world and us.

Separate is a horizontal term. It deals with those on our level-people. Being received by God is a vertical relationship. It goes up to heaven. Keep a distance from those who are not like God. Keep your horizontal relationships straight. If you mess up your horizontal, then the vertical will be messed up too. But if you keep the horizontal right then the vertical will be right and that's how you make the cross. Once you do you've got to get up on the cross to separate yourself. It will require you to humble yourself and let things go that you like. Afterwards you will have a sacrificed life.

A sacrificed life is evident to everyone around you. When you are really honest with yourself you can walk uprightly in the anointing. Then when you show up around people who are living in sin, they automatically shut down and change their conversations because the light has come around them. That's the conviction of the Holy Spirit and the anointing upon your life. If you can walk around sinners on a regular basis and that doesn't happen, then you should be concerned.

As His children God has given us a challenge, but the choice is yours. He said it's time to stop running from the light and let it hit you. Do you really want to come to the light? The darkness can't comprehend the light. The light shows up the deeds of darkness. But it will also purge you and take you to a higher level than you have ever gone before. However there are a couple of more areas you have to master before you can be thoroughly purged and become the person God created you to be. One is the flesh.

Conforming Images-the War Within

For everything in the world-the cravings of sinful man, the lust of the
eyes and the boasting of what he has and does-comes not
from the Father but from the world.
(1 John 2:16-NIV)

You've got two bodies, a spiritual and a natural body-celestial, and terrestrial. The human body is composed of three parts-the spirit, soul, and body. Your spirit is your conscience, that part of you that lets you know when you are right or wrong. Your soul is your mind, the will and emotions. And your body is the part of you that you have to bathe, shave, dress, and feed. It is the exterior part of you that covers your spirit. It is the part that grows, lives and dies. When you become a Christian you are born again. However, you don't return to your mother's womb and become an infant again like Nicodemus suggested in John 3:1-9. Physically, that isn't possible. What actually happens is that your spirit is born again, but your physical body and your mind remain the same. You now have a quickening spirit in you. You know Jesus and the power of His resurrection here on earth. You'll know Him in our spiritual body, not your natural one. If you are 5'8" before you recite the prayer of salvation, you will be 5'8" when you finish praying. If you liked fruit before you recited that prayer, you will like it after you finish praying. The only way you will see any changes in your mind and physical body is to wash your mind in the Word of God. When you do this, your mind will be renewed and your habits and actions will conform to the Word of God because your body takes its instructions from your mind. This is an ongoing process.

You have a choice. You can either be led by your renewed mind, which is led by your spirit man. Or your flesh-your carnal physical nature, can lead you.

If you ever find yourself doing things that you know you shouldn't do, and you want to stop but you don't know how, then your flesh, your carnal nature is dominating you. Sometimes you are in it so deep that you can't even see that you're sinning. If darkness is rooted in you it will keep you blind. Maybe you just know that you are in a situation you shouldn't be in and you want to get out. Or perhaps the light did shine on your secret affair with darkness but you still can't find your way out of that web of deceit. That means you need more light in your life, and you finally realized what God was trying to keep Adam and Eve from discovering in the Garden of Eden.

When God told them not to eat of the fruit it wasn't that He was a dictator or trying to be mean. The fruit came from the tree of the knowledge of good and evil. It doesn't matter whether it was an apple, a pear, or whatever. What did matter was that he gave them a choice. It was a choice to obey or disobey. If they obeyed they could continue to live in dominion, power, authority, luxury, paradise for the rest of their lives. However, if they chose to disobey they would know evil.

He didn't want them to know evil. The word know is the same word used in the Bible when it said that Adam knew Eve. Adam was intimate with Eve. God didn't want them to become intimate with evil. When you become intimate with evil you become aware of the struggle within. Paul describes that struggle in Romans 7:18-20. He says,

"I know that nothing good lives in me, that is, in my sinful nature. For I have the desire to do what is good, but I cannot carry it out. For what I do is not the good I want to do but the evil I do not want to do-this I keep on doing. Now if I do what I do not want

to do, it is no longer I who do it, but it is sin living in me that does it."

In other words Paul is saying that he wants to do what is right, but because of his nature to sin he is constantly struggling with that issue. In other words, there is a war within.

Adam and Eve never knew that struggle until they ate from that tree. Because of their decision to disobey God, every human being born on the face of this earth is intimate with that struggle too. Sin passed on to every man, woman, boy and girl. Now we all struggle within. We will always have that conversation with the devil. We continue to try and see how close we can get to the fire. If God's Word says, "Thou shalt not covet…," (Exodus 20:17) we want to sit down and look at that item for a long time, but we stop just short of coveting it. How close can we get to the line? That's the sin nature that was passed on to us.

Keep in mind the word knowing. God didn't want us to know good and evil. The word know is an intimate word. God didn't want us to be intimate with evil. We weren't created to know evil. While they were in the garden, Adam and Eve only knew good. They knew God. Once they went to that point that they were intimate with evil, there was another element that they had to fight. It caused a war within. When Jesus died and rose again He gave you the power to win that war. You've got the power to do it, but do you use it?

Supernatural Beings

In 1 Corinthians 3:3, Paul rebuked the church. He said,
"You are still worldly. For since there is jealousy and quarreling among you, are you not worldly? Are you not acting like mere men?"

The fact that he says they are *"…acting like mere men,"* implies that they aren't *mere men.* They are children of God. God's children have the deposit of the Holy Spirit, the Spirit of the Living God residing on the inside of us. That means that we are not normal. A child of God isn't supposed to act like normal people. We're not mere men.

We must refrain from ordinary responses. If we restrain ourselves from sin we are abnormal. But if we go along with sin that means we're acting normal and we're under the control of ordinary impulses. It's ordinary for you to respond when somebody talks about you. God said you've got to hold your peace and wait for the right time to respond. If not, you're acting ordinary. If somebody can get you upset just like that, you're acting ordinary. God said if His peace isn't controlling your mind you're acting ordinary. We've got this thing that we say, "I'm only human, that's why I act the way I do." But according to God's Word you can take that word and throw it out. We're not supposed to act human because we are supernatural. We've got a supernatural Holy Ghost on the inside. A supernatural God died for us so we've got supernatural power to live in this natural life.

Demolishing Strongholds

How much more, then, will the blood of Christ, who through
the eternal Spirit offered himself unblemished to God,
cleanse our consciences from acts to lead to death,
so that we may serve the living God!
(Hebrews 9:14 NIV)

By now you are probably saying to yourself, "I get the point. But how do I get out of this secret affair with darkness? I'm entangled so deeply in this web." You have got to break the enemy's stronghold on your life. So what is a stronghold?

A stronghold is a philosophical structure. In other words, it is the way you think. It is the foundation upon which you base your values, opinions and ideas. In the natural realm a stronghold is a rock that has a cavity in it. It is hollow on the inside. But you have to find your way into it. You could look at a bunch of rocks together, but you couldn't tell which one has the cavity in it. You have to go underground to get to the cavity. A stronghold can't be detected with the natural eye. So when the enemy looks and sees rocks, they just see rocks.

When David was hiding from Saul in the caves of Engedi he was hiding in strongholds. That's why none of Saul's men could tell where David was. If there is an area of your life that you have been warring with, it is probably a stronghold. That means that there is a mindset, an opinion, a set of values or ideas that you believe in; and they convince you that it is all right for you to continue in that particular pattern of behavior. Yet it stands firmly embedded in your mind, in opposition to God's Word. Anything that tries to come up against the knowledge of God must come down, because the weapons of our warfare are not carnal, but mighty through God to the pulling down of strongholds. Anything that causes you to not be fully committed and purged unto God is a stronghold that has set camp in your mind. It has made its mind up and said, "I'm not moving." And it's going to take war to move it. You just have to make up your mind that you're ready to fight until you pull that stronghold down.

Only the truth of the word can start demolishing the strongholds. And once one stronghold goes down, then the ground starts clearing and you can begin to see others go down that you didn't even know were there. The word will tear down anything that exalts itself against the knowledge of God. Listen to this. If the knowledge of God says that you are supposed to trust the Lord and wait, then you'd better wait. Don't try it out. Those strongholds mess up your consciences because now your consciences don't even feel what God is saying. So God is saying I've got to purge your consciences.

When there are strongholds in your life you need the Holy Ghost to hit the target and show you what they are. Only He can point them out for you. You may think it is one area of your life when it could be another. You don't have time for decoys. You might be fighting more than one fight. You don't have time to fight none fights. I'm going to fight this fight that I'm supposed to fight. And that's it. I'm not fighting none fights.

God said if you pray I'll show you that stronghold and you can hit that target. So God shows us the right one, but it seems so small that we say, "No. That's not the one." You see, the devil hid it from us. We can't see it without the help of the Holy Spirit. But we still want to get to that one over there because it looks so exciting. Actually, the only thing that can detect the strongholds in your life is the Word of God.

Sometimes you can be reading the Scripture and all of a sudden something pops inside of you. It will cause you to say, "Man, I didn't see it like that before." The Holy Spirit just revealed an area in your life where the devil had a stronghold on you. And you know what you do? You leave it alone. But you ought to stop right there and say, "Thank you God. That was the thing that got me messed up right there."

You see, the Holy Spirit sees the things coming at us that we don't see. He sees how strongholds develop in your life even when you can't. One way they develop is when the human body goes through a process called Sensory Adaptation. This is when your body's sensory receptors are only being stimulated by one particular type of stimuli. If it happens on a continual basis that will be the only stimulus your body responds to. In other words, whatever you expose yourself to is what you will respond to. After constant exposure to one particular stimulus, your body will ignore all of the other stimuli and develop an appetite for that one stimulus.

All your sense organs retain receptor cells that are especially sensitive to one type of stimuli. And they aren't receptive to certain things if you have deprived your senses of them. You can look at the TV, but when you look at the Bible you get sleepy. If you're used to getting a certain kind of touch your body will crave it. You can't fight the flesh now because your cells are sensitive to that. They work from your nervous system. That's why you can't fight it any more and you yield to temptation. Americans are exposed to 15,000 sex scenes by various types of media; 41 of them are shown on television each day. We're not just talking about posters or magazines. If you are exposed to sex that many times a day, that's why you are drawn to it. Now when that kind of thing happens you don't know how you are going to respond to anything else.

That's the way the devil works. Women come to church with tight dresses on while men come with their shirts all unbuttoned. The worship is just with people who want to be seen in front of people. Before you know it a little cussing word here or there doesn't bother you. A little touch here or there doesn't bother you. A little stealing here or there is tolerated. There's sin all in the house. Your flesh just has to have it. Strongholds can develop in your life like that.

Another method is Sensory Depravation. This is the elimination or reduction in sensory stimulation by oppressive interrogation procedures or brainwashing. It occurs when you are systematically oppressed or interrogated. This is one of the methods used in prison camps when captives are tortured. The goal of the oppressor is to deny your senses of what you know you're supposed to have and make you comfortable with what is given to you. You are deprived of what is rightfully yours.

That's what the devil did to the children of Israel while they were in Egypt. When they first got there they lived on the best land and had the finest Egypt had to offer. Then after the king and his aides died, the new administration was not familiar with Joseph's family and how God delivered the world from starvation through him. So they simply saw the Israelites as a threat, intruders to their community. First they began to deprive them of the privileges that they enjoyed when they entered Goshen. After doing that for a while they told them that if they wanted the basic necessities of life they would have to become slaves. By that time the children of Israel had lost sight of who they were. They accepted the Egyptians' terms and were slaves for almost 400 years. And it all began because the Egyptians were able to change their mindsets. The Israelites were caught in a stronghold.

That's why when the Israelites got out of Egypt they wanted to go back. God had delivered them out of Egypt, but they refuse to let Him deliver their minds. They chose to hold on to the fears and degenerative thinking that they used to survive while in Egypt. Only Joshua and Caleb had the faith to see who they really were and what God had in store for them. It wasn't until 40 years later that the next generation understood that they were supposed to live in the best land and have the best that life had to offer. They had a different mindset. The oppressor didn't let them know that they were kings. If you don't know who you are you need to be delivered from your mindset. It's time for you to come out of Egypt.

The word oppressed means "to force and crush." Egypt forced them and crushed Israel. They crushed their spirit because they couldn't think. This is the same thing that happened with Balaam when he was riding his horse. The horse that Balaam was riding pushed his foot against the wall and crushed it. That's the same word that was used there. And the word also means "double." That means that Egypt had given them double distress. Egypt not only had their minds, it had their bodies too. If I've got your mind, I've got your body. I could tell you what to do if I get your mind, and your body would obey. That's why the word says you need to get a brand new mind.

The whole spirit of Egypt was to divide. That's why it was called Egypt because the word means "to split and divide." The delta end split the southern part, and it was split straight down the middle by the Nile. If I can doubly depress you, or get you to feel bad in your mind then your body will follow. If I can make you feel like you aren't healed, after a while your body is going to listen to your mind. If I can make you feel like you're broke you will predict what you do and you will live out just what you are. If I can keep making you feel like that's what you're supposed to go through you'll continue to live like that. If I can keep making you question, "Why is everybody else getting blessed while I'm not?" I'll make you start talking like that and I'll make you start living what you are talking.

Egypt was definitely the enemy's tool. His method of operation was to divide and conquer. It isn't anything new. That's what he's been doing all the time. He's also been effective at doing that in the church today. What do you think the word denominations means. It means to divide the one nation into multiple parts. His purpose is division. It's not about a denomination. It's who we are in Jesus.

It's time for us to stand up and take back what God has for us. If that means we need to purge all of the sin out of our lives then that is what we must do. God will help us. When you really start living right God will get in between anything that hinders it. Live in the power, not talk in the power. You can't have a Pentecost unless God cleans something up. Don't you listen to anyone who tells you it's going to be all right? You better get it cleaned up. How are you going to put up with sin? You watch all that sin in the movies and on TV. If he can put the sex and perverted things in the home and on TV he's got you. You are letting your receptor cells be drawn that way. That's what happens to people who look at pornography.

Psychological domination is another tactic the devil uses it on us to put us in strongholds, but he must use a vessel in order to get that done in your lives. It could be a person, a car, money, a boy or girlfriend. You are in opposition with God because you are not fulfilling what God said you are. You are waiting for someone else to tell you who you are, to define you or your status when God already told you who you are. And you are waiting for an outside influence.

When that domination comes the enemy lays back. You only know when the struggle is over and you are in a stronghold. Yet the weapons that will be used to pull down the stronghold are in your mind; you can't even see them with your eyes. You can't even touch what I'm depositing in your spirit with your hands. It is intangible. You must use it to demolish what the devil has placed on your life through years of time. Now you are not fighting with sensual weapons. Take the bibs off and eat that hard meat of the Word.

Once you get this concept you aren't ever going to get into

opposition with God. You're going to run back to God every time to get what you need. See your (carnal) psychological appetite needs to get destroyed and God needs to show you what a good taste is. A good taste is something that you can't put your hand on. It is the intangible. It is hidden in your heart. You have a word that's hid in your heart a will not and to sin against God. This word will pull you out every time. And you won't be thinking about what others think, or your imagination. What the television man said, or what they said at the convention won't concern you. You are going to handle this situation from the Word of God. You can't mess with a saint who's got the Word and knows how to pray, fast and live right. All of a sudden you are armed and dangerous. Some Christians talk about they are armed and dangerous, but as soon as a trial comes they can't pray their way out of a wet paper bag. But I'm talking about you being a Christian who, when the situation gets rough, you get a word from God. And it will break the stronghold because the anointing destroys the yoke.

Psychological domination is when an outside influence subjugates, makes you his subject. That influence subjugates the mental atmosphere, which leaves the imagination open to be violated. And the response of the will is more favorable to an action or an event of the outside source rather than to the knowledge of God. That's a stronghold when somebody outside of you has got more influence on you than the Word of God. And your mental atmosphere is more subject to how they control you. If your TV controls you more than the Word then you are in a stronghold. If this habit that you have is still satisfying, and you have to submit your will to fulfill the habit, you are in a stronghold. Don't you know your will can be controlled by the devil without you even knowing it?

You know why some people don't have their purposes yet? God only gives you your purpose if you are controlled by Him. (Matt. 4:10) The devil uses you to fulfill his will. See, it's illegal for him to jump up out of the spirit world and move here on earth without using a body. That's why he uses you and others to do his work. The devil said I need to talk about this sister on this side of the church, but I need to use you. I hate this sister over here and I hate you. I've got to put somebody in a stronghold so I can control him.

Satisfaction is the devil's greatest weapon. Only something that satisfies you can put you in a stronghold. The thing that satisfies you is where your stronghold is. That's where he gets you at, but you don't know it. The devil doesn't want you to be around anyone who tells you the truth. If you are around anyone who tells you the truth you are going to be dangerous.

You get inside a stronghold when people make you feel good and don't tell you the truth all the time. That's why your preacher can't always tickle your ears. He needs to tell you the truth so you can get free. You want a preacher who will make you feel good. That's why we've got people shouting in churches every Sunday and they aren't free. Let me tell you something, the devil doesn't care about anybody shouting in church on Sunday. But he hates for some body to shout who has the Holy Ghost. He doesn't care what you do, just as long as the power of God isn't with you.

Some people had a problem because we were up in here doing the Holy Ghost electric slide. But you see I don't have a problem when somebody does the electric slide and they are in here enjoying themselves in the Lord. They are living right and they are trusting to get it together. But I have a problem with those who jerk and fall out yet they are the biggest liars; they are phony. They just live all dirty. What is the style of a dance going to change in you? That's a Christian facade. If they come to church and they want to slide, let them. But some people are so stuck in religion. They say, "That's what we are used to. That's the old-time way." The old-time way almost killed me. Don't come to church with all that religion. That's nothing but a stronghold.

Watch what you expose yourself to. When you're living right your receptor cells won't receive anything but what agrees with the

Word. You've got to have some God around you. You have an appetite for it. You've got to have it. You need Him, and that's a good thing. You see, God wants you to have an intimate relationship with Him.

Psalms 51:7-11

7   Purify me with hyssop, and I shall be clean;
      Wash me, and I shall be whiter than snow.

8   Make me to hear joy and gladness
      Let the bones which Thou hast broken rejoice.

9   Hide Thy face from my sins,
      And blot out all my iniquities.

10   Create in me a clean heart, O God,
      And renew a steadfast spirit within me.

11   Do not cast me away from thy presence,
      And do not take Thy Holy Spirit from me.

NAS

Intimacy with the Father
*How God anointed Jesus of Nazareth with the Holy Spirit
and power, and how he went around doing good and healing all
who were under the power of the devil, because God was with him.
(Acts 10:38- NIV)*

Go back with me for a moment to the Garden of Eden, if
you will. When God created man His purpose was for them to
have fellowship with Him. Remember, the Bible says that He
walked with man in the garden in the cool of the day. They had an
intimate relationship with God. He had some things to share with
man then, and He has some things to share with you and me now.

Even though the devil has secrets of darkness, God gave you
secrets of the light to keep you alive and strong. His secrets are
found in His Word. And when you develop a relationship with
Him, He reveals them to you in your private times. David said, thy
words have I hid in my heart that I might not sin against thee. You
see, when you hold His Word in your heart, it strengthens you and
destroys the strongholds that keep you in bondage and prevent you
from receiving everything God has for you. You'd better make sure
you keep a hold to your secrets and don't let your secrets go. God
has something precious and inexpressibly important to give to you
and I that our familiar pattern of the normal devotions can't accom-
modate. The problem is that we don't know how to worship anymore.

God can't give you something different if you do the same
things all the time. Worship is not just to open up your bibles, sit
down and look at them. Because if He gives you something differ-

ent you might think it wasn't God. The Bible tells us that the things done in the Old Testament were types, shadows and signs that represent what God wants to do for His people in the New Testament. In the Old Testament we find that the children of Israel never entered God's presence without worshiping and praising Him. As a matter of fact, they didn't do anything without worshipping and praising God. Before they went to battle they sent the singers out. When they marched around the walls of Jericho the singers and musicians were in the lead. It was the praise and worship that ushered the power of God into their situations. When we learn how to worship and praise God His power will show up in our situations too.

There are so many things that God has in store for His children. He wants to give us the desires of our hearts. There are things we have been waiting for and desiring for a long time, but we haven't been in the position to receive them yet. If we will get into position we can receive them. But there have been things standing in our way.

See God is saying, "I'm trying to get to you. But there are things in the way-lust, disobedience, and your will. Move those things out of the way. All you've got to do is surrender your will and God will be able to get to you. God is still standing in line waiting for you to move those things out of the way so that He can get to you. You may have been hurting for a long time. But just wait on the Lord, for surely, He's coming. The thing you've been waiting on for a long time is there for you. God wants to get it to you.

However, He has to purge you so that you will be prepared to live and enjoy the life He has for you. Some of us aren't enjoying life. We don't even have what we need. Yet, a million dollars isn't anything to God. You're telling me that the world is supposed to have more than God. The people who you get your phones from, the large businesses and corporations are billionaires-AT&T, UPS.

No way. Deuteronomy 28:1, 2 starts out by telling us that if we "…fully obey the Lord [our] God and carefully follow all his commands …God will set [us] on high above all the nations on earth. All these blessing will come upon [us] and accompany [us] if [we] obey the Lord [our] God." Then it goes on to list the blessings for the next twelve verses.

It's not that God can't do it. We just haven't been in the position to receive it yet. The people of God are supposed to come together with one mind and do what he told us to do. When we do that we will see what we have been looking for. We serve a good God. You didn't have to beg God to wake you up this morning, to keep that bullet from hitting you; you don't have to beg God for money. God is in the position to give; now you just have to get into the position to receive.

This may even be a new step to you. You may even be considering doing something that you have never done before in your relationship with God. But that's good because in order to get something you never had, you have to do something that you've never done.

You may be used to just going to church on Sundays, and perhaps in the past you thought that was enough. But, if you really want everything that God has for you it will require something more. You have to have your own relationship with God. That means spending time with Him by reading, His Word, studying and praying. See, you can't get that good something if you don't practice doing it. The popular sports figures can tell you that. You'll never be able to pray if you don't practice praying. Prayer and fasting is work because your body doesn't want to do those things. Even if you want to think the way God wants you to think, it is so important for you to spend time with Him.

I've learned that you can't depend on someone else's relationship with God. The world will think you lost your mind, or you cracked your mind. You're mad. You're crazy. No, that's not how it is. You just woke up that's all. When you cracked your mind the light came in through the crack. Now you've found Jesus for yourself. Tell the Lord, "Crack me God so the light can get in. Change my mind." Then watch what happens. When you start praying and depending on the revelation from the Holy Ghost you will have   continual revelation, not just every now and then. The more you spend time with God the more you will get to know Him. You'll find that you see God in another way everyday.

In your intimate times with God give up the secrets that aren't like Him. This is the gentle part of the purging process. As you bathe in His all-encompassing love, you'll see habits fall off of you. He will bring everything you give Him from the spiritual to the physical. He'll meet each of your needs and you will see it in the physical. Whenever you look in the mirror, you will look more like your Father every day. You'll develop such a love relationship with Him that you won't be able to wait until you can get alone with Him again. If you are married, I'm sure you can identify with this example. I travel sometimes. And when I am away I call home and speak to my wife. Our conversation might go something like this, "Hey, how you doing?

She says, "Hey."

"I've been thinking about you."

"I've been thinking about you too."

"I can't wait till I get home to see you."

"Yeah, I can't wait till you get home. I wish you were here right now."

"I'll be there after while."

Then when I get there the excitement, the adrenaline starts pumping up. The king is back home and he's coming home to his queen.

When you're not where you should be with God you have been away for a long time. Yet He misses you, and He wants you back. He says, "You've been out there a long time with your mind lusting on things."

You should be saying, "Yeah Lord, I sure have. I can't wait till I get back home."

God will say, "I can't wait till you get home too."

Then God comes in and says, "The king is coming."

Then when God comes in, what you've been thinking about all that time is what He has waiting just for you. When I get home with my wife, what we've been thinking about all that time is what is in store for us. We take it from the mind and the spirit and we bring it into the physical. We let God bless us in our fellowship.

Develop an intimate relationship with the Father. He's waiting on you. There is so much He wants to give you. The next time you say, "I'm hungry," God will feed you. The next time you need something to wear, He'll send someone to clothe you. Stop violating the characteristics of the anointing. See you violate the characteristics of the anointing when you entertain conduct that doesn't glorify God. So the next time you meet with the Lord He won't have to push you to say amen. The next time you get in trouble, you'll just have to open your mouth in faith and know He's going to answer. He'll say, "I'm here."

You don't want to be like Saul. After He disobeyed God the anointing departed from him. He wasn't getting any new revelation. So he was living off of old manna. Worms were growing in it. And that old stuff got into him. He stopped getting the word from God. He went to familiar spirits. He didn't pursue an intimate relationship with God. David on the other hand sought the Lord. In Psalm 27:8 tells us that David's heart's desire was to seek God's face. The silent part is what spoke back to God.

You see, God is after the heart. Your issues come from your heart. When your heart speaks back to God then you are living in the abnormal. Study before you speak, so you'll speak from your heart. What comes out of the heart is the real you. And God can see what's in your heart even before you make it known to others. It's time for us to be real and tell the truth. No matter who you are, as long as you live you will have to pray about things that are in your heart. I've got to get down on my knees and pray about stuff in my heart too. God looks on the hearts of men, not their actions. That's why He wants an intimate relationship with His children, heart to heart. And it is through this relationship that you are purged. You see, in order for you to be purged God has to have a loving relationship with you. It's an intimate thing. He doesn't purge anyone whom He doesn't love. He doesn't put fire on anyone He doesn't love. He purged Israel because He loved them. God told Israel, "I'm going to burn you up every time you live out there in sin. You're supposed to be my people."

How would you feel if your spouse paid more attention to someone else than you? She was spending all her time over there. How do you think Jesus feels when we just want to stay dirty, when the devil can seduce us any kind of way? How do you think Jehovah feels when His children aren't living holy inside His faith? Don't tell me that something's not going to rise up in you. God won't let you be traditional when you have the Word of God shut up in your bones. It's just like fire. We might as well make our minds up that we are going to live right.

It is obvious to God when His children aren't living right. It shows in their behavior and speech. They say and do things that give them away. Take for instance Adam and Eve in the Garden of Eden. After they ate from the forbidden fruit God came to the spot where they always fellowshipped and they weren't there. So He called for them because they were hiding from Him.

God asked Adam, "Where is that intimate place we had before? I came here today and you weren't at your spot? We used to have this relationship. What happened?" Adam said, "I heard your voice and was afraid. I hid myself because I was naked."

God knew that he had to be intimate with somebody because

the entrance of intimacy is through the ear. That's why any marriage that doesn't have communication isn't going to make it.

God's question to Adam was, "Adam, you were the head. Who told you that you were in poverty, sick, depressed, I didn't. Who told you that the devil was more powerful than you? I didn't. Did you ever hear me say that you weren't supposed to have authority? What kind of intimacy are you having because you know evil now? You never knew evil before, but you know evil now." So He asked, "Who told you that you were naked? In our conversations that subject never came up."

When you are intimate with sin, you will begin to think like the devil wants you to and not like God does. Satan deceived them and they lost sight of who they were. They forgot who they were in God. "That's all I knew from the beginning." They lied to me. I knew that stuff from the beginning but forgot it. What did Adam become afraid of, God's voice? Adam why don't you like my voice any more? Did; my voice sound good to you before? Are you scared of my voice? Why because you had intimacy with evil? You were never afraid of God's voice before. A good sounding voice doesn't sound good to you any more. A good sounding voice that tells you that you're a king, you don't' like that anymore. But after having intimacy with someone else he would rather hear the voice of another, the confirmatory bias to receive somebody else's belief system over mine. And then when something happens and you make this one mistake, you take this one mistake and say, "Well I guess it has to be that way cause that's how I am." But that's not the truth. I'm just trying to wash you and get that mess up out of you. The belief system is my voice. It was in the cool of the day that God came. But because Adam was in sin God's voice sounded like fire.

Once God starts purging you, you are going to forget that you were broke. You will forget that you were sick and the problems that were around you will become small in comparison to His power. You will remember God's goodness and blessings. God will purge you with His fire.

Fire was never meant for His people. The reason you've got to be baptized with the Holy Ghost and fire is so it can burn all the evil out of your life. Fire was originally for the devil. When he comes around you he needs to see fire. He'll see the Holy Ghost in you and it will just remind him of where he's going. When you start speaking the devil starts saying the same thing that Adam said, "I was afraid and I hid." The reason he hides is because your voice starts sounding like fire to him.

When God asked the woman what had she done, she said, "The serpent outwitted me and tricked me; he seduced me, and cheated me out of the truth." And let me tell you what he took. He tricked her and didn't let her enjoy Adam's voice. And he made her feel like he'd be a better man. He told her that she would be like God because she just wanted to change her position of authority. If she had been like God she would have lost her position. It's time for you to get into line with God's Word. You need to declare war on all voices that aren't God's. Get intimate with the voice of good. It's sketched in stone. God knows and is intimate with every one whom loves Him.

Now the only thing left for us to do is to choose to conform. He chose us before the foundation of the earth. It's up to us to chose whether or not we want to be chosen. Some of us use our free will to violate the One who gave us our free will.

Job 23:8-10
But if I go to the east, he is not there; if I go to the west, I do not find him.
When he is at work in the north, I do not see him; when he turns to the south, I catch no glimpse of him.
But he knows the way that I take; when he has tested me, I will come forth as gold.

Purged by Fire

But when God has tried me I should come forth as pure gold. Purged into His purpose. When we get purged we need to get a release of all unwanted things in our systems. We need to do it regularly, systematically. Get rid of any unwanted data in our systems- anything that isn't like God, our own personal feelings, and personal desires. All of the information is being removed and He's filling you with knowledge, dynamite, power from heaven, understanding so that you can acknowledge that God is God.

You must free yourself from contamination. I can't hear God the way I need to hear him until I get purged. When God speaks His Word there is always a thought behind the word that brings forth a true meaning to what the word really says. It is revelation and you get it from meditating on the Word. The thought is more powerful than the surface meaning of the word you just heard. The word you heard on the surface is like a seed that goes into the ground. When the seed goes in the work is being done out of everybody's sight. No one else can see what the seed is doing on the inside. People may not see what is going on with you. Deep in your earthen vessel there is a treasure that is hid. And this treasure isn't of our power, but it is by God's Power.

And after a while this work that's going on inside of you will be birth. And this work will come forth the more I clean myself, and purge myself. Once you see my blessing start to burst through my earth it might come up like a little leaf. But you don't know the end result. So you be careful how you judge people when there is nothing happening. Don't count them out. You just don't know what's going on. You may not understand the speed of my results. I'm just in the planting season, but my harvest is coming. I might look a little strange right now, but just watch me. You might count me out till ten. But I might be down until nine and jump up on ten. The reason that I jump up on the last count-ten-is so that you will know that it was God who did it. A miracle would have burst out. The reason I would have jumped up on ten is because if I had jumped up on two or three I would have done it myself. But when I jumped up on ten you knew that God did it. You may take a picture in the light but it is developed in the dark. See what was happening, it got developed in the dark. I might look a little sad right now, but that's all right because my glory is coming.

God's got to speak to you by His Holy Ghost. There will be some sad, hurting, lonely, days when you get purged. Because God is hitting something that no one else knows about but you and Him. You could be in a crowd and then you start to feel like there's nobody there but you and the Lord. And when He starts hitting that spot you start feeling like everybody knows what's going on. So you want to be cool because you don't want anybody else to know.

Sometimes you could be in a conversation and everybody's talking and you say, "Oh yeah." And you didn't even hear a word they said because God had you in a place right there, and He was working on you. All of a sudden you knew there was something on the inside of you saying, "God just keep talking. Just keep talking." And what God is doing is He's got that fire just sitting there musing. Then somebody asks you, "You alright?" And you say, "Yeah, I'm fine." To them you are fine but you know what? You all of a sudden feel like you've got to get by yourself. You really want to get into the presence of the Lord. You need to pullover on the side. You need to do something. And sometimes when you feel something and you really want to get into the presence of the Lord, David said it doesn't matter where you go, He's there. You can hide from the crowd, but you can try to get away from your problem-the thing that God is working on in you. You see, you can try to escape it, but you aren't going to get to your purpose until you get clean. I repeat, you're not going to get to your purpose until you get clean.

Once you get clean, the measure of your cleanliness determines the outpour of power in your purpose. If you've got enough power going on you'll be all right. Take a microphone for example. The system means nothing without the power amps. Without sufficient power given in the strength of the speaker (the person talking) it would put a strain on the amps and make the power amplifiers strain. We need 3000 amps for the bottom speaker and another 3000 for the top one. If you clean your vessel and there's not enough power coming through your vessel it will cause your vessel to break down. You can't get the power to flow until your vessel gets clean. Because if the power of God flows at that level and your vessel isn't clean His power will kill you. With the flow of that power coming through at that magnitude you'll lose your mind because you don't have the capacity, the intelligence, or the Word to handle it. Your vessel has to be able to handle the flow. So when you get enough Word coming through you can handle more work for Jesus. If you can't get your work done because you need some more cleanness that's all right. God is prepared to give it to you.

The play game with you is over. People can see it on your face. One side of your face looks all right. The other side says, "I know the game is over." See, you're split. You're divided. Once the game is over you will be made whole. Jesus never asked people, "Do you want to be half?" The whole thing has got to come together.

Do you really want to be clean and fulfill your purpose and be what God designed you to be? Do you really want to be what God made you before you were formed? You see in order to be what God made you before you were formed you have to go inside that realm that's not formed and see what you are supposed to be.

2 Timothy 2:19 says, "Let everyone who names the name of

Christ depart from iniquity." There are vessels of gold, silver, wood, and earth. Be a vessel unto honor, sanctified and fit for the master's use and prepared unto every good work. Fit-meet- just as God made Eve for Adam. I've got to be fit to be used by the master. In other words, if He's going to use me I've got to be fit. It doesn't make a difference what it feels like. He just can't just use me! What are you fit to be used for?

There are vessels that are dishes. Yet some of the vessels are used for trash. Some are used for honor. If you purge yourself from evil you will be a vessel fit for the master's use. If someone holds himself aloof from these faults he will be a vessel held in honor, dedicated and fit for the master, ready for any good work.

You've got to get honest and be straight up with yourself. If you are calling on God you must avoid evil. Is there any appetite in me that loves evil? If that's the case then you need to say, "That's where I need to be purged. I know God that you say I'm not supposed to do this." The Word of God says that sin has pleasure only for a season. Church people are too religious and don't want to be honest. Yet God is in us, and He's looking at us. Still, we're not being honest with Him. That's tradition and religion. You know something's going on inside of you. But see if you really got it together you don't need any help from God.

See we try to appear that we've got it together. Once God gets us out we've got to say, "I'm not going back." The question is do we enjoy Egypt? Do we enjoy letting somebody feed us and tell us what to do? We don't enjoy the freedom in Jesus? Don't be entangled in the yoke of bondage. And the yoke of bondage says, "Do what I say." But freedom gives you liberty in Christ.

You must enjoy the freedom in God. Where the spirit of the Lord is there is liberty. (2 Corinthians 3:17) The Spirit of the Lord, this means where Jesus is your lord. It didn't say where the carnal feeling is at, and the part time feeling is at. It said where the Spirit of the Lord is. And when it says where the Spirit of the Lord is that's just what it meant. If you've got the spirit of the Holy Ghost and Jesus is reigning as Lord that's where your liberty is on you. The same Spirit He had to rule and to conquer is the same Spirit that's on you. If anything tries to overtake you, you have the Spirit to conquer, to demand, to say stop or go. When you have the Spirit of the Lord you have the spirit to be a lord. If there is bondage on you, you have the Spirit to command it to stop.

Vessels of Honor

*"If a man therefore purge himself from these, he shall be a
vessel unto honour, sanctified, and meet for the master's use,
and prepared unto every good work."*
(2 Timothy 2:21)

If you purge yourself you will be a vessel whose appraised value
is wealth to Him. God will say, "I need that vessel right there
because it is clean. I can use this vessel. I can turn the world upside
down with this vessel." And if it is precious to Him, He won't let
anything happen to His vessel, no matter what. That's God's vessel
and it is one to honor. Not only is it honored, but it is sanctified.
It's a vessel that is set aside and appraised with honor, but it is sanctified and set apart from profane things. This vessel is set apart to
God. God will look at you and say, "I'll take this vessel."

I don't know if you noticed or not, but there is a process going
on here. This vessel first gets clean, then it is honored-I've got a
value on it. Now I'm going to take it and then it is set-aside for
God. Now I have another vessel, this one is honored and sanctified. There is an extra special spot for this one. It's not only honored, it's sanctified. This vessel is getting closer and closer to God.
The deeper you go in the process, the purer you become. The
purer you become, the closer you get to God and the more valuable you become to him.

There are some key words in this scripture that you may want
to focus on. The first is honor. The first part of Timothy's name
means "to honor." It means to honor God. When something is
sanctified, separated from profane things and dedicated to God;

that means that it is going to be set aside. There is a special spot for this vessel. I have a special place for it. There are two parts to the process. In the first part of the process you are set away from profane things. In the second part of the process, then you are set apart unto God.

The next word is to *meet*. The word means "thanksgiving and good grace." It also means "profitable." God wants you to be meet for the master's use profitable-pro-fit-able. This vessel is meet; it is pro-fit-able. The husband and wife must agree before they get married. Pro-fit-able- "powerful, to fit, before it even gets there." This vessel is powerful to fit before it even steps inside to do what it needs to do. You'll be prepared already. God said if you go ahead and purge yourself you will be powerful to fit before you go into anything that you go into. It will bring out the best. Use is, the owner's purpose. So when you say that you want to be a vessel of honor, sanctified and fit for the master's use, you are actually saying that you want your relationship with God to be so pure that He sees you as one of His most valuable treasures.

Unfortunately, a lot of folks want to start doing stuff before they make it through the entire process. That's why they jump in as soon as they get a little honor. Well they've got honor but they aren't sanctified yet. Then they can't handle the honor. The first thing that's got to happen when you get a little honor is you need to get humble. Some get honor then they get a little big headed. That messes them up. I've seen it happen like that.

Then there are some who get honor and follow the next step by getting sanctified, and they become holier than thou. Now you aren't fit with power before hand. So that will mess you up too. But when you get the right order-honor, sanctified, and meet-you are fit for the master's use. Now you are ready to be used for the owner's purpose. And He can fulfill in your life what he created you to do. God won't use you until you do all of that. You might as well do what God says. Pace yourself. Lay aside ever weight that is slowing you down, and become intimate with God. Who told you that you were supposed to have weight on you anyway? God didn't. He said His yoke is easy and His burden is light.

As a matter of fact, His burden is so light that He established a day of rest for us. We usually rest at night. There is nothing unusual about that, but as I was studying the creation in Genesis 1, I realized something I have never seen before. God created the heavens and earth in seven days. "God called the light 'day' and the darkness he called 'night.' And there was evening, and there was morning-the first day." Gen. 1:5, 8, 13, 19, 23, 31; 2:2. On every day God had and evening and a morning. On the seventh day there was no evening. Now the seventh day is the day that you are supposed to lay back and chill out and let God do the work. It was rest all day. You're still in the 5th and 6th day. You're supposed to rest in God on the seventh day. You are to rest in God all day on the seventh day.

While you rest in Jesus it is always daytime. You're trying to work it yourself instead of letting God handle it. His grace is sufficient so that the power of Christ can rest upon you. If the power of Christ is resting upon you then that means that there is not a moment when the Power of God is not upon you. When the Power of God is upon you it's always daytime. That's why the devil can't take you out. While you rest in Jesus it's always daytime. Are you getting sanctified to the point where, "I'm not trying to work that thing? If God did that for Adam what am I trying to do? Why should I try to change that thing?" The 7th day means completion. I don't know why He didn't write an evening on that day, but isn't it great to know that God's got your back so that you can rest? All you have to do is keep your vessel pure before the Lord.

Another important point for you to remember is that you must purge and not be intimate with evil so that you can hear His voice. God speaks to those who seek Him. If you are intimate with God you won't listen to anybody else but Him. Do you realize how powerful one Word from God can be?

> *"He will sit as a refiner and purifier of silver: he will purify the Levites and refine them like gold and silver. Then the Lord will have men who will bring offerings in righteousness." (Malachi 3:3-NIV)*

The Strength of God's Word

For these commands are a lamp, this teaching is a light, and the corrections of discipline are the way to life.
(Proverbs 6:23-NIV)

When the centurion came to Jesus to ask that He heal his servant he said, *"...Just say the word, and my servant will be healed."* (Matthew 8:8 NIV) He knew the Power of one Word from God. Psalm 107:20- "He sent His word and healed them..." That's just what Jesus did. And the servant was healed that very hour. He understood that one Word from God on the matter was all he needed. God's word can do exactly what He said in your life. You don't need to see the thing that God prophesied about you because you have a sure word of prophesy. You've got it already because you heard it in the Word. You see, *"...It is impossible for God to lie..."* (Hebrews 8:18) When He speaks it has to come to pass.

You've got the word from God on your situation. When He has tried you, you'll come forth as pure gold. Oh, you might look rusty now, but just wait until He gets finished. Malachi 3:3, says,
"He will sit as a refiner and purifier of silver; he will purify the Levites and refine them like gold and silver. Then the Lord will have men who will bring offerings in righteousness."

When He is finished with you, your life will be an offering of righteousness to the Lord. God is cleaning up the things hanging around in you that aren't any good. He is purging you with fire. You see, God's fire purges without consuming you.

In Exodus 3:2 the Bible tells us that Moses saw something that attracted his attention. As he was keeping his father in law's sheep

Purged Into His Purpose

he saw a bush that was burning but it wasn't consumed. When he went to take a closer look, "There the angel of the Lord appeared to him in flames of fire from within a bush. Moses saw that though the bush was on fire it did not burn up." (NIV) Within Moses there was s desire to see the Israelites free. He said I'm tired of looking at your people in bondage. God was glad to hear that because He was tired too. So He told Moses to go the Pharaoh and tell him to let the Israelites go. God has placed some desires inside of you that will lead you to your purpose. Yet they will also let you know that He did not create you to be in bondage. Just like God burned the bush without consuming it, the fire of the Holy Spirit will purge your conscience unto good works, without killing you. He's burning everything around you except your purpose. He's going to shake everything loose that isn't right.

When silver gets tarnished it needs to be brightened. Once you scrub something long enough it gets hot and that heat caused the dirt to melt off. God is going to be like a goldsmith. He's going to clean, scrub up, and burn until it is pure. He wants the cry of your heart to be, " Purge me with hyssop and I shall be clean. Create in me a clean heart and renew a right spirit in me." (Psalm 51:7) once you get clean, the only way to stay clean is to continually shine the light of His Word on your life and fellowship with Him. The Bible tells us that if we cover our sins we shall not prosper, but the person who confesses his sins shall have mercy. You must confess in order to get clean and then you get mercy. (Prov. 28:13)

If we are going to be a reflection of Jesus in everything we say and do, we are going to have to be holy. The Bible tells us, "Thus saith the Lord, be ye holy cause I am holy." God said it's time to get it together. Sometimes when you are in the fire you are so uncomfortable that you want to know, "What is it that I need to do to get God off of me like this?" God will keep you in that furnace until you get burned. He'll say, "I won't move until you move. You need to get it cleaned. You need to stop your bad attitude; stop

68

spending that money; stay away from that girl cause she will make you fornicate; stay away from that man cause he'll make you commit adultery." Get your face right; get it scrubbed so you can get the wrinkles out of it. God wants to put a smile on your face. Once you start getting clean a whole lot of things that looked a certain way aren't going to look that way any more.

That's why God hasn't given some people some things yet-mate, money-because you're not clean and you can't receive it yet. He knows you can't handle it yet. If He gives it to you, He may not be able to get it back out of your hands again.

While God's fire is purging you He is also trying to develop some character in you. Romans 5:3,4 tells us "We rejoice in our suffering, because we know that suffering produces perseverance; perseverance, character; and character, hope." When God begins to purge everything that is not like Him out of you, He also wants to put in characteristics that are like Him.

In order for us to receive everything that God has to give us we will need to possess certain attitudes and habits. God can't give you a promotion on the job if you aren't diligent in the position you currently hold. He can't make you a leader if you have trouble following those in authority over you. He won't give you a bigger house or a better car if you don't even take care of the one you have. All too often we look for a quick fix. You have to understand that if it took you years to get into this situation, it may take you quite a bit of time to get out. Now that's not to say that God doesn't deliver people instantly, He does. But sometimes He wants to deliver you slowly so you can see the process. He wants to show you exactly what steps you have to take to come out of that mess so that He can strengthen you as you go. If you will stick out the purging process, you will find that it is well worth it in the end.

God loves us unconditionally with an everlasting love. Now when you love someone that much it's hard to stand by and watch them make the wrong decisions without stepping in to correct or assist them. That's the love of a father. And He is also a jealous God. His jealousy is different from ours. Do you think God is going to allow you to treat Him any old way and then leave Him and after all that He has done for you? People will say that He wasn't able to deliver you. His jealousy is revealed as a consuming fire. In Ezekiel 36:22-26 God tells His children,

> *"This is what the Sovereign Lord says: It is not for your sake, O house of Israel, that I am going to do these things, but for the sake of my holy name, which you have profaned among the nations where you have gone. I will show the holiness of my great name, which has been profaned among the nations, the name you have profaned among them. Then the nations will know that I am the Lord, declares the Sovereign Lord, when I show myself holy through you before their eyes. For I will take you out of the nations: I will gather you from all the countries and bring you back unto your own land. I will sprinkle clean water on you and you will be clean; I will cleanse you from all your impurities and from all your idols. I will give you a new heart and put a new spirit in you; I will remove from you your heart of stone and give you a heart of flesh."*

See God wants the world to see His goodness and power operate in the lives of His children so that He can draw those sinners to Him. He wants to draw them by His goodness. It's time for us to get to the place where we draw men unto Him. Even though we are going through something we are not distressed, perplexed, not in despair. Your life should be a light for some body to see how to get out of trouble, for somebody else to go and grow on. Some body should be able to look at your life and see the direction that they need to go in. But some people look at your life and don't want what you've got. There ought to be an irresistible grace on your life. Grace is that thing that enables you to be what God wants you to be. When people look at you they've got to say, "You may rub me wrong, but one thing about you is that you always challenge me to be what God wants me to be." Remember, the most important thing that we can do in this life is win souls to Jesus. It's all about souls.

Sometimes however, God's people aren't the lights He's called them to be. They ignore Him until they get into trouble. Then when they are in trouble they can hear Him speak really well because they finally take out the time to sit and listen to Him. There are even times when He will lead them into trouble to get their attention. (Matt. 4:1) You see, God doesn't want any lukewarm Christians. Lukewarm just won't do. God would prefer that you are cold rather than lukewarm. He said make up you mind. You must break up that fallow ground and keep the fire burning. Luke 3:16 tells us that John's baptism was a baptism of water, but Jesus' was one of fire. The fire purges the sin out of the way. When sin comes up out of your life stay in fellowship with God and the angel of the Lord will chase it away for you just like he drives away the chaff in Psalm 35:5. He will assemble the wheat, not the chaff.

One way to remain strong in the Lord after you begin the purging process is to get together with other believers. Forsake not the assembling together with the saints. (Heb. 10:25) You can't get the resources and the blood flow that you need in order to cleanse you of your sins if you stay away from the house of the Lord. He'll assemble you in His storehouse, where he dwells and reserves things. As you fellowship with the saints you will find that not only will they be an encouragement to you, you will edify them too. Stop being around people who don't want to challenge you to live right. Stop being around people who make you feel comfortable living in your sin. Once you start hearing the word it will make you do something about your life. And fellowship with believers will be a source of strength to you.

As you become more consistent in your relationship with God, the study of His Word, and fellowship with believers you will begin to know the power of His resurrection. Then you will be made

conformable unto His death. That means that you've been prepared by the heavenly Father to attain what He has for you. I'm on
the way to that level. Paul said I haven't reached the mark but I'm
striving for it. I'm not worrying about what happened yesterday. It
can't help me today. If I keep thinking about what happened yesterday it will keep my mind on what's going wrong, or what caused
me to sin. And focusing my mind on that will make me stay where
I'm in the present and hinder my future. You've got to forget those
things that are behind and reach for the prize of the higher calling.

Don't take the regular call. If the call is not beyond you, don't
reach for it. It's got to be beyond your resources, your means, and
what you can think about. Look, I'm telling you He is able to do
exceedingly abundantly above what you can ask or think.
(Eph.3:20) You can't even calculate what He can do. It is above
your ability to ask. In other words, whatever you open your mouth
to ask or think, He can do past that. There are some things in your
mind that you've thought about and He said, "Listen, I'm able to
do above that." But you limit yourself. Some people say, "I want
my thirty fold, sixty fold, a hundred fold." God's not even limited
to a hundred fold. He just said a hundred fold so that we could
understand where He's coming from. The problem is you reach the
point of what you can do. You are always supposed to reach past
yourself. Your goals are too short. I'm talking about a BIG God.

God wants to purge your conscience so that you can think past
yourself. God said it's that stuff on your conscience that's got you
thinking low. Your conscience has you messed up so you started
thinking what people want you to think. And that limits you. You
can't even fellowship with God like you're supposed to. You think
that God wants you humble, and He does because He will not
share His glory with anyone. But the humility that we see is a false
humility. Humility isn't walking around like you are nobody.
That's why I don't sing that song that says, "For such a worm as
I..." You aren't going to find that in the Bible. How's God going

to call me that?

People are walking around saying, "I'm so humble in Jesus." Did it look like Jesus let anybody come up to Him and tell Him just anything? Jesus was humble, but you've got to understand what humility is. Let me tell you something, the kind of humility Jesus was talking about was being what God said you are. If you're not doing what God said you are, that's pride. When you don't obey and call yourself a king, that's pride. If you aren't living like a king or a queen, that's pride. But once you start walking in your kingship and queen ship that's humility. Because that's who God said you are. The Bible says humble yourself under the might hand of God that He may exalt you in due time. Does it sound like He exalts the mentality of bums? No He exalts he mentality of kings. He lifts you up. Stop settling for a crowd that wants you to go around and do the same thing. If you are in the same place you were last year, you ought to make up in your mind; look it's time to change. Something's wrong. But we are too hard headed. We just want to satisfy our friends. And God says, "Pay attention."

That's why we can't get through to God. We've got all of that stuff in our conscience. And our conscience is that part that comes back and starts talking to us when we open up our mouths and say, "God is able to do what He said He can do in my life." Yet your sin conscience comes back and says, "You don't have it."

God told you to keep on talking. You've got to start opening up your mouth. God wants us to purge ourselves from this low estate that we've been thinking about. We are somebody in Christ. We are the royal priesthood. We have an immortal Christ living on the inside of us. And He is ours right now. He wants us to enjoy it here on the earth. Yet we accept the downhearted stuff. But we must go past the inside of us. You've got to pay attention to your intentions. If you intend on being great, you've better pay attention to it. You sit back and you have an intention but you don't go forth with it. But if you have an intention to be great for your own intentions, you'd better pay attention to that too. The Word of God is sharp, powerful, a two-edged sword and is a discerner of the intents of the heart. If you want to find out your intentions you need to get in the Word and the Word will show you your intentions. Don't let a prophet or anybody tell you that they are discerning you and they didn't get their Word from God. Stop putting your money in people who you know aren't right. Pay attention to their intentions. Allow God's Word and peace to guide you in your decisions to give. If God said don't do it yet, then listen. God told you to be a steward over that money. He will hold you accountable.

You are not only accountable for what you know about God's Word, but what you say. Abraham was smart. He understood the power of his words. That's why he spoke in faith. He didn't even stagger. He was strong in faith. In his mind he had a picture of Sarah having a baby. All of this was written for the Christians today too. If there is anything in your mind that causes you to be offended, Jesus was raised up for your offenses. If there is anything that causes you to see yourself in a wrong way, he rose for that reason. So He justified you too. Romans 5:1 says, *"Therefore, since we have been justified through faith, we have peace with God…"* (NIV) Why are you distracted? You aren't supposed to feel down. You have access; you've got what you need because you don't have the devil's mind. You have God's mind. Therefore you've got peace. Now, you're rejoicing in the hope, and enjoying yourself. You will see the picture in my mind come to pass. It is coming. There is an expectation because God's Word is sure.

Abraham was called the Father of our faith because he believed even though he couldn't see it. When we face insurmountable obstacles, we need to look to God in faith. Faith is the ability to think of ways to deal with difficulties and problems. Once you get faith, then your faith has to have an imagination. You start thinking of ways that you can deal with this. You become a strategist in the Holy Ghost. You learn how to fight. Don't just sit back and take what the devil's putting on you. Don't take it lying down.

Imagination is the power to create pictures of reality with your mind in words. It is the power to create a way out, and see yourself in the picture, but you've got to speak it. See you've got to see yourself in the picture, and you've got to say it with your words. It is the ability to get you a husband, create a healing, and become a millionaire. The more you open your mouth and paint the picture that's inside your mind, the more it becomes a reality because you did it with your words. You've got to open your mouth and say what you see. You can't accept what somebody else says out his or her mouth to you. (Hebrews 1:3) Abraham said I know that He is able to perform and give Sarah a baby. I am exactly what God said I am. Can't you see the picture in your mind? See yourself delivered. I see myself coming out of the stronghold. The stronghold isn't the picture that God gave me. That's not the picture. That's not what was created on the inside. That's why I've got to come out. I've got to fulfill the picture He gave me.

Jesus was the image of God. He was a picture before He even got here. He is the express image of God. This Jesus is upheld by the Word of God's power. If God's Word can uphold Jesus, then the authority of God's word will hold together your picture. The pieces in the picture have got to come together. Create the reality with your mind and start speaking it with your mouth. That's what father Abraham did.

It's going to hurt when God demolishes your stronghold. When He blows it up there will be some effects from the bomb. Then the effects cause you to say, "Well, I don't feel like it today." But God said, "That's not what you were supposed to say. You weren't supposed to think like that. I've got to blow up that vocabulary that causes you to paint the picture that you are in now. You use your mouth to get in sin; you've got to use your mouth to get out. You've got to open your mouth and confess. To get saved you opened you mouth and confessed that Jesus Christ is Lord. You're going to have to open you mouth and confess that where the Spirit of the Lord is there is liberty. And if the Spirit of the ruler is in me, therefore, everything else must become subject to the Lord that's in me. It's got to be demolished. *Subjugate* comes from *su- yogam.* Sub means under; *yogam-* means yoke. *Subjugate* means "under a yoke," Your mind activity is under a yoke. If you want to get out of a situation you've got to yoke that thing to Christ. God said take my yoke cause my yoke is easy. If you yoke that thing with Christ you'll get out of that situation. Speak to that situation that's giving you a problem. Tell it, "My Christ." That means it is under the subjection of Christ. The anointing that's in you puts everything under the subjection of Christ.

You can't stay in sin because the yoke is supposed to be under your feet. But you haven't seen yourself on top of the problem yet. And you can't speak your way out of a problem until you see yourself out of it first. When you begin to see yourself with your feet on top of the problem you can't stay where you're at. Your mind won't let you because you've started painting yourself a picture with your words. I got married by words. Before my wife and I got married we said, "We are going to get married." White dress, we saw it. Coming down the altar-we saw it. You start paying attention to your intentions. When the plans start getting out of sink you yoked it. You say, "I've got to make some plans, oops, that's not coming out right. I've got to get that back on track."

Imagine if somebody told you, "You can't make it without me." What would happen if you start to believe them? Men start rapping with girls because they see themselves with the mental picture. And we didn't just see ourselves walking down the street with her either. And you start talking to her. You didn't see yourself sitting on the couch. You saw yourself engaged in a relationship with her. And depending on how far ahead your dream is concerning your relationship with her, you start making plans to get to that goal. Sometimes it got us in trouble, but we must reverse it.

What do you think Jesus is trying to do with us? He comes and drops an image of you, "Here it is, bam!" You've got to see yourself in the ultimate goal. Don't just see yourself on the way. God will show you the goal, and then He'll put you right back there on start. Then He blows up all the bridges so you don't know how to get there. And He tells you that you're going to have to pray everyday to get there. God will say, "That's alright, because the dream was too big for you to get there by yourself.

That's right you can't make it by yourself. So you're going to have to talk to me. Keep talking. Talk some more. I'll show you how to do it next week." He'll show you how to do it. If you have a dream, purge your conscience continually. God's not going to give you a dream unless you do what He says.

DNA = Duplicate Never Again

*"They made the plate, the sacred diadem, out of pure gold and
engraved on it, like an inscription on a seal:
HOLY TO THE LORD."*
(Exodus 39:30 NIV)

Sometimes you don't find out who people really are until God calls them home. When you are in your purpose you are effective. You are the best you, you can be. We like to feel important. We want to be in one ministry when God said you should be in another. Foreknowledge and predestination are important to purpose. God placed in your spirit a picture of who you are. The goal was that God would have a community of first fruit heirs. If the first fruit is blessed then the whole is blessed too. God wants to have a community of originals. You can't reproduce an original. You can only get the first fruit of something once. You are trying to copy someone else when you should be an original. We want to be important, but that's not purpose. Some times we feel important because we sit in a certain section of the church all the time.

God made us superior to any other community. You might as well get used to that term. So if you want to be like somebody, copy off of Jesus. If you are controlled you aren't a part of the superior community. 2 Timothy 1:9 tells us that He called us with a holy calling according to His own purpose and grace. Which was given us in Christ before the world began. That's the pro-thesis. God said that He needs us to fulfill the purpose in His mind because He's not coming back down here. Even when Jesus returns to get us His feet will not touch the ground. We're going to have to come up to Him. The rapture. Only on His second return will His feet tough the ground. (Zech. 14:4) You can't get there until God gives you the mind and abilities to do so. We have this treasure in earthen vessels that the excellency of the power will be in God, not us. We don't have a money problem; we have an anointing problem. If we have the anointing we will have everything else.

A pro-thesis is that which is set before in a spoken discourse before it is proven, based on original discovery. God said something about you before He proved it. And He said it based upon an original discovery. He went all the way through and came back and said, "Yeah, they're victorious. They are called according to my purpose." In other words before you were even in the womb God said, "Prophet to the nations." He said that about Jesus. The prophets kept saying, "Jesus is coming." Yet He wasn't even here. What HE said He can perform. God said some things about you. He put you in your purpose and said it before you even got into it. HE's said some stuff about some people who still aren't where they are supposed to be at yet. He already spoke it. And if He said it then He can perform it. See you ought to put more trust in what He said and not worry about whether He can perform. You see, His word is on the line. If He performs something and never said it that doesn't make a difference. But if He speaks and never performs then there's a problem. If God called you and said you will be a blessing, then no body can stop it, He's got to perform it.

When God called you HE spoke and put a purpose in you. I was preaching before I got here. The reason I know this is because my mother and father saw me preaching before I got here. Before we even came here we were already here. The problem is you've got to try to get back here and see that you were there. God told them, "This is the deal. He's going to be preaching. He's going to be a pastor." My father said, "you're not going to be playing only music boy. Get it together. Not just music. It's not going to work." My father saw my purpose before I was. I was created to fulfill it.

Some people say, "I was running from God. I didn't really want to preach." Don't even tell anybody that because what was happening was you weren't running from the Lord, you were being stupid. God said this is what you're supposed to do. Now that I know that this is what I'm supposed to do I'm just as happy. I know people who have struggled with God's call, but why? Struggle? What are you doing struggling? This is what God called you to do. If He called you to do something it should be a sweat less anointing. If you ran from God you haven't seen what you are supposed to be yet.

Before you got here He had someone to have intercourse. That's why there are no illegitimate babies, just illegitimate parents. Out of 500 million sperm, God chose that particular sperm to make you. When you came forth, God spoke. When the egg went to the sperm God said connect. And everything that is in you now was in you when He said, "Connect." When you really find your purpose you will stop working for people.

If you have drudgery on your job, and are having a hard time it's because you aren't in your purpose. You won't have drudgery in your purpose because God put everything in you according to your purpose. HE gave you everything you need on this earth right now so that you could fulfill your purpose. The design was in it. Therefore you would not have to go to anybody else to get it. All you have to do is listen to His call. He was just cleaning me up just so I could hear what He was saying. You're going to get the right mate, the right purpose. He's going to fix, clean up your families because He's put the anointing in you. You are called according to His purpose. Acts 16:31 He said the whole house has got to get saved. I need to get exactly what God wants me to have. In the sperm is DNA= Duplicate Never Again.

We've got churches that try to Xerox the presence of God. But you are an original. You don't need to be a copy. Nobody's going to see a copy. They only want to see the original. Be original. I'm trying to tell you what God put in you. And sometimes you know full well that you have an anointing-another level in you- but you're denying it because you're just trying to please people. Those people didn't call or create you so they can't give you your purpose.

Let me show you what will happen when you don't know your purpose. When people don't know their purpose the design is despised. They don't fit. Look at what happened when Solomon became king. This is what happens when others don't know your purpose. They despise you and try to steal your dream. These two women had babies out of wedlock. They came before Solomon to dispute whose child it was. Two people have a dream. One person's dream is dying and another's is alive. The person whose dream died is trying to take yours. Yet they can only do it while you are sleeping. Don't lay back and let it happen. You can tell people who are trying to steal your dream, they don't care if it dies or not. I'm pregnant; I've got a baby coming up. I've got deliverance. Solomon represents the Lord, or a man of God; and the sword represents the Word. The word is a discerner of the intents of the heart. You need to know how to see the Lord in situations. A mother's spirit knows how to make a decision to keep things going. But the father's spirit knows how to protect it. You need to know how to make decisions in your situations.

See if you aren't careful, if you are in a situation and you're not doing what God told you to do, before you know it you can become the oppressor. You will use the same type of spirit that the devil uses on you. But when God puts purpose in you, you don't have to do that. Act 10:38 Oppression messes with the mind. If I can oppress you I've already got you. I'm using tactics on you to brainwash you. I'm showing you that you can't step across that line. I'm using punishment to prove to you don't step over that line. Because our minds have been oppressed. But if you make the right decisions you can step across that line. Hosea 4:6 my people are destroyed because of the lack of knowledge. The reason you have financial problems in your life is you lack the knowledge to go through it and get it. If the marriage is struggling you lack the knowledge in taking care of it. If you are sick you have got to have the knowledge in order to recover. It is according to foreknowledge.

The shepherd's job is to feed you with knowledge and understanding. If you get the knowledge you can get out. Yet you want to stay home; you don't want to come to church. What you are saying is you hate knowledge. That's why the devil can whip you up because God's people lack knowledge. Once you understand that the devil does not have the freedom to come in your house and tear at you, he can no longer do that. Once you get that knowledge that God doesn't want you in lack, you won't have it. First you must have the knowledge.

People get ripped off if they don't have the knowledge in an investment. What area am I having problems in? The ignorance of my decisions is what put me in it. That's why now, in order for me to get out, I've got to get out through knowledge. Unfortunately, the church is trying to get caught up in the experiences. You can't overestimate the event. The process is what is important. If you made a decision the course was set. So in order to get out you've got to use knowledge to come out of the course. The problem is that some of us want it to happen overnight. God said it doesn't even work like that. You enjoyed that thing a good while; you've got to come out the same way. I'll give you some grace, just like He gave to the children o of Israel. They were supposed to stay in Egyptian bondage for 70 years and He cut it down to 69. That was only because Daniel saw in the word of God that it was the year of jubilee, the acceptable year of the Lord. There is an acceptable year of the Lord always going on with you. Ecclesiastes says to everything there is a season and a time. You've got to make sure that when the time comes for your purpose you have got to make sure that you are in the fullness of time. And once you are in the fullness of time for your purpose, then you are in your season. If you go before your time you aren't in your season. If you go forth before then the time wasn't mature enough for you to be released. It wasn't in the fullness of time. That's why you end up in situations.

I'm in situations because of decisions. Proverbs 13:18 tells us that you only know what you've learned; and all that you learned isn't all there is to know. Poverty and shame shall be to him that refuses reproof and disregards instruction. We thought we knew and we had a hard head. If you are in a difficult situation you should listen to the advice given to you. Either you pay now and play later, or you play now and pay later. Proverbs 28:19 says that one who tills his ground shall have plenty of bread. If you hang with people whom all they do is lack and have dreams, they are going to drain you too. If you work diligently, you will have plenty of bread. People have learned to do that from the world's system, and then they continue to do that if they keep getting over with it. This verse uses the word vain. The person who chases fantasies, something that is not real will never accomplish anything. A person who fantasizes always talks but never does it. Then the reality finally hits. And all they can do is talk about what they did 4-7 years ago. They haven't accomplished anything since then.

Decide that you will do what the Word tells you to do. Prophesy and pray and you will see what the Spirit reveals. Till your spiritual ground. Break up the fallow ground. Let that seed go in there and plant the Word. That scripture didn't have anyone's name aside it. It didn't have any particular type of people by it. If you do what the Word says you will have what it says. It says that, "I will have plenty. If I do this I shall have plenty." Personalize it. But the problem is, we don't put God on point like that. We just ride by, read a scripture and don't pay it any attention. God said that is what I said; those are instructions. If you follow my instructions, stop hanging out with dreamers, people who aren't going anywhere. Or you will be in poverty. When you know your purpose you are free.

Free to Pursue Purpose

If the Son therefore shall make you free, ye shall be free indeed. But solid food is for the mature, who by constant use have trained themselves to distinguish good from evil.
(John 8:36-NIV)

I've got liberty, freedom. You see, once I know my purpose you can't hold me down. No one can hold me down. (2 Corinthians 3:17) Somebody who is broke isn't free. This scripture says, "Now is the Spirit of the Lord Supreme in Authority. And where the spirit of supreme authority is manifest through the power of decision, there is freedom." Timothy Moore Version (TMV). God is in Supreme Authority. And this is wherever He is. So if I decided that I'm going to be just like God, I'm free. You said one thing, but because God is with me and He is Supreme in Authority, I'm free. Opinions can't hold me down. If you walk with God you are free. Deliverance isn't freedom. Some people are delivered but they are not free. A lot of people have been delivered and aren't free. They can come back Sunday after Sunday. Freedom is the weighted responsibility to have the liberty to dominate. You are supposed to dominate. I've got the liberty to tell the devil, I'm not sick, I've got food on my table, etc. I've got the Supreme Authority with me. So I will open up my mouth and change the course. Amen! Amen! Amen!

It was for freedom that Christ set us free. And don't let yourself be burdened again by the bondage of domination. Domination is bondage. Luke 4:18 you've got to understand that you've got kingship in you. Everything he did I let him do it. If I've got the strongman with me, Jesus, then the devil shouldn't be able to do this in my life. It was my decision to do it because I didn't get the knowledge to fight him with. I'll eat it another day. Some people get free and then they want to go back. According to the text, when Jesus went to preach to them the cell door was open. He had to go and tell them, come out. The door has been opened. He had to ask them, "What you still doing in there? The door is open. Come out. The Bible didn't say that he went to set them free; He went to preach deliverance. He went to preach. The spirit of oppression had made them think that they would continue to be dominated. How many of you have been free but scared to come out? When Christ died, you got free instantly.

(Hebrews 9:14) Now that your conscience has been purged from dead works and you are serving the living God you can no longer walk in the darkness of the past. You must go forward and walk in the light. 2 Peter 1:9 says, He who is in denial by failing to develop these qualities is concealed spiritually from sight. He is nearsighted and powerless against sin in the future. He's forgotten to take hold of the truth. (TMV) We are in the forming stages of an embryonic blueprint. You can't get to His purpose until you are purged from sin, and you will continue to be purged until you die. Some of us have lords in our lives and they aren't Jesus. Romans 8:28 tells us that there is a purpose for our lives. There is a purpose, but whose purpose are you going to live? Purpose is a prophetic thesis about your life. The introduction of a book is the thesis of the book. Don't get stuck in one chapter in your life. That's not the only chapter in the book. The pro-thesis already said what was going to happen in your life. People try to judge you on chapter five when God had to put you through chapter five to get the foolishness out of you so that you can get to chapter six. But they are still stuck on chapter five because they think that's where you are going to stay. However, when they come to find you the next time you're no longer in chapter five, you have skipped to chapter nine. Now they don't know what happened in between there so they have got to be nosy and create something to fill in the gaps.

Sometimes you have got to answer people. To answer is to discern. To speak by discernment. It is a declarative response to the unspoken thoughts of the heart. Sometimes you have to respond to people based upon the stuff that they don't really say but it is in their hearts. You need to answer that stuff that they aren't saying. Pharisees were questioning John and trying to put him on the spot, asking if he was the Messiah. John said, "Oh, I caught you in that plot." Luke 3:16 - John said I only baptize you with water, but the Messiah will baptize you with the Holy Ghost and fire. He will thoroughly clean His floor. When I get in there that room will sparkle.

In that same scripture he said that he wasn't worthy to untie Jesus' shoe laces. When you talk about somebody's shoes you talk about purpose. Whenever you put somebody's shoes on you've got to be big enough to fill them. John said I can't even get Jesus out of His shoes, (purpose). Have you been baptized with the Holy Ghost? If you are living in sin and are comfortable you have not. If you can run your mouth and have a dirty mouth you have not. If you can stay in the sin state that you are in and lay your head down and go to sleep then you have not been baptized by Jesus Christ and you have not been immersed in His fire. If you can still sip upon the can then you have not. If things bother you, if you worry about stuff and they take more precedence than God, then you have not been baptized in the Holy Ghost.

I want to see some gold. I'm tired of seeing people who all they want is wood on them. That burning bush represents humanity to me. He will burn everything out of you and not consume you. See the problem is we don't really want to get that close encounter with God. We want that distant encounter with Him. You think that one baptism will take care of everything. But you've got to get a filling daily. Every day get in His presence and get filled daily. He gave you a Bible too. Sit down and read your Bible and see it for your-self. Fire will burn chaff. Angels are present when fire burns chaff. (Psalm 1- whole chapter) The winnow throws up the wheat and the chaff. But the wheat stays when the wind blows the chaff away. But that good stuff, the wheat falls back down and stays by the person who is throwing it up. And His name is Jesus.

Now the ungodly are like the chaff, which the wind blows away. If there are some ungodly things in you God will burn it with unquenchable fire. That is the fire of hell. So if you are living like hell and you aren't getting that chaff off of you, that stuff is pulling you closer and closer to hell. And God is saying, "It can't dwell with me." Chaff represents hell. As long as you've got chaff on you, you will be sad, and you'll stay broke. God is looking for some people who have fire.

How slick have you been? Neither is there any creature that is not manifest in His sight but all things are naked and open unto the eyes of Him of whom we have to do. See, the problem is you just want to have a little dab will do you church on Sundays. You don't want to get in His face and say, "Help me Lord, forgive me. Wash me." You don't want to moan. You want someone to lay hands on you and set you free. But God says I'm here. Get close to me. I'm the goldsmith. I've got the fire. This fire is inextinguishable fire. You're powerful when you get baptized in the Holy Ghost. When God gets through with me I'm coming forth like gold.

Scriptures to Meditate on

For a will and testament is valid and takes effect only at death, since it had no force or legal power as long as the one who made is alive.
So even the [old] first covenant (God's will) was not inaugurated and ratified and put in force with out the shedding of blood.

1 Corinthians 2:4
My message and my preaching were not with wise and persuasive words, but with a demonstration of the Spirit's power.

Matthew 13:7, 22
Other seed fell among thorns, which grew up and choked the plants.
What was sown among the thorns is the man who hears the word, but the worries of this life and the deceitfulness of wealth choke it, making it unfruitful.

Psalm 119:105
Your word is a lamp to my feet and a light for my path.

Proverbs 9:17
Stolen water is sweet; food eaten in secret is delicious! But little do they know that the dead are there, that here guests are in the depths of the grave. (Sheol)

Philippians 2:5

Your attitude should be the same as that of Christ Jesus.
Hebrews 11:24-25
By faith Moses, when he had grown up, refused to be known as the son of Pharaoh's daughter.
He chose to be mistreated along with the people of God rather than to enjoy the pleasures of sin for a short time.

Psalm 101:1-8
I will sing of your love and justice; to you, O Lord, I will sing praise.
I will be careful to lead a blameless life-when will you come to me"
I will walk in my house with blameless heart.
I will set before my eyes no vile thing. The deeds of faithless men I hate; they will not cling to me.
Men of perverse heart shall be far from me; I will have nothing to do with evil.
Whoever slanders his neighbor in secret, him will I put to silence; whoever has a haughty eyes and a proud heart, him will I not endure.
My eyes will be on the faithful in the land, that they may dwell with me; he whose walk is blameless will minister to me.
No one who practices deceit will dwell in my house; no one who speaks falsely will stand in my presence.
Every morning I will put to silence all the wicked in the land; I will cut off every evildoer from the city of the Lord.

1 John 2:27-28
As for you, the anointing you received from him remains in you, and you do not need anyone to teach you. But as his anointing g teaches you about all things and as that anointing is real, not counterfeit-just as it has taught you, remain in him.
And now, dear children, continue in him, so that when he appears we may be confident and unashamed before him at his coming.

Ecclesiastes 12:13-14
Now all has been heard; here is the conclusion of the matter: Fear God and keep his commandments, for this is the whole duty of man.
For God will bring every deed into judgment, including every hidden thing, whether it is good or evil.

Acts 26:18
To open their eyes and turn them from darkness to light, and from the power of Satan to light, so that they may receive forgiveness of sins and a place among those who are sanctified by faith in me.

James 3:15-18
Such wisdom does not come down from heaven but is earthly, unspiritual, of the devil. For where you have envy and selfish ambition, there you find disorder and every evil practice. But the wisdom that comes from heaven is first of all pure: then peace loving, considerate, submissive, full of mercy and good fruit, impartial and sincere. Peacemakers who sow in peace raise a harvest of righteousness.

Proverbs 14:23
All hard work brings a profit, but mere talk leads only to poverty.

Job 4:30
Is there any wickedness on my lips? Can my mouth not discern malice?

Exodus 3:9
And now the cry of the Israelites has reached me, and I have seen the way the Egyptians are oppressing them.

Hosea 4:6
> *My people are destroyed for a lack of knowledge.*
> *Proverbs 13:18*
> *He who ignores discipline comes to poverty and shame, but who-ever heeds correction is honored.*

Proverbs 28:19
> *He who works his land will have abundant food. But the lone who chases fantasies will have his fill of poverty.*

Hebrews 9:11-14

11 But when Christ appeared as a high priest of the good things to come, He entered through the greater and more perfect tabernacle, not made with hands, that is to say, not of this creation; 12 and not through the blood of goats and calves, but through His own blood, He entered the holy place once for all, having obtained eternal redemption. 13 For if the blood of goats and bulls and the ashes of a heifer sprinkling those who have been defiled, sanctify for the cleansing of the flesh, 14 how much more will the blood of Christ, who through the eternal Spirit offered Himself without blemish to God, cleanse your conscience from dead works to serve the living God?

NAS

**For book orders, other teaching series or information
write or call:
Life Music Publishing
Po.Box 13291 Baltimore, MD. 21203
or
Life Music Christian Fellowship
3407 Belair Road Baltimore MD. 21213
410 325-4100**

Published by

1.800.249.4427